Your Employee Brand is in Your Hands

How Any Employee Can Create & Promote Their Own Personal Leadership Brand for Massive Career Success!

Your Employee Brand is in Your Hands

How Any Employee Can Create & Promote Their Own Personal Leadership Brand for Massive Career Success!

Lisa Orrell, CPC

The Generations Relations & Leadership Expert

SPEAKER • TRAINER • CERTIFIED LEADERSHIP COACH
AUTHOR • THOUGHT LEADER

Intelligent Women Publishing
A Wyatt-MacKenzie Imprint

Other Books Written By Lisa Orrell

Boomers into Business: How Anyone Over 50 Can Turn What They Know Into Dough Before and After Retirement (2011 – Intelligent Women Publishing, a Wyatt-MacKenzie Imprint)

Millennials into Leadership: The Ultimate Guide for Gen Y's Aspiring to Be Effective, Respected, Young Leaders at Work (2009 – Intelligent Women Publishing, a Wyatt-MacKenzie Imprint)

Millennials Incorporated: The Big Business of Recruiting, Managing and Retaining the World's New Generation of Young Professionals (Second Edition 2008 – Intelligent Women Publishing, a Wyatt-MacKenzie Imprint)

Please Note: *Lisa's books can be purchased on Amazon in both paperback and Kindle versions, as well through other large online book retailers in print and e-book formats.*

Dedication

This book is dedicated to the fabulous family & friends that support me every day, through thick and thin, such as: My amazing son, Jenner (Mama loves you, Bubba!); my adoring Dad, Papa O; my loving Mom; and my wonderful partner, Dr. Erin K. O'Neill and the O'Neill Family.

I'd like to thank my long-time Publisher, Nancy Cleary, Founder & President of Wyatt-MacKenzie Publishing, Inc. This is our fourth book together and it's always a fun ride with her!

And I'd also like to dedicate this to all of you employees out there who are willing to do the work it takes to achieve your personal career goals as well as make a positive impact on the world & workforce. Go for it!

Your Employee Brand is in Your Hands:
How Any Employee Can Create & Promote
Their Own Personal Leadership Brand
for Massive Career Success!

By Lisa Orrell, CPC
The Generations Relations & Leadership Expert
Certified Leadership Coach • Personal Branding Guru
Speaker • Author

FIRST EDITION

ISBN: 9781939288080

Library of Congress Control Number: 2013931499

Intelligent Women Publishing
A Wyatt-MacKenzie Imprint

TABLE OF CONTENTS

What People Have to Say about
Your Employee Brand is in Your Hands

Due to the legal policies of many organizations, the full names of individuals and/or their employer's company names were required to be withheld in some of the following testimonials.

"Most consumers prefer to buy brands that we know, like, and trust. In many cases, we're also willing to pay more for those brands. Yet most of us don't think of the fact that in our places of employment we have our own 'personal brands'. Some of those brands are positive, some are neutral, and some are negative. So if you want the people making the decisions about your career and compensation to know, like, and trust you then you need a positive brand, and this book will show you exactly how to make that happen."

Steven Rothberg
President & Founder of the Niche Job Board: CollegeRecruiter.com

"Lisa has been a featured speaker at our Annual Summits for the past three years and she always delivers! And when she educated us on Personal Branding at our Leadership Summit this year our audience of 400+ people went nuts. They're still talking about her presentation and how valuable it was. She is a TRUE expert when it comes to developing a Personal Brand at work so this book is a must-read for anyone who cares about their career growth!"

Winn Claybaugh
Co-founder, Owner, and Dean of Paul Mitchell Schools International Motivational Speaker & Author of: "Be Nice (Or Else!)" BeNiceOrElse.com, PaulMitchellTheSchool.com

"As the Founder & President of a content marketing and digital PR consultancy for organizations with products that target job seekers and/or employers, combined with being a former Career Coach, I am highly aware of the fact that employees need to be focused on their Personal Branding to excel in their careers. And Lisa's book clearly maps out how to do it; not only to get more recognition at work, but in your industry. It's also a great resource for job-seekers to obtain clarity on 'who' they are so they can pursue positions and employers that will be a good fit with their Personal Brand. Lisa's book definitely 'comes recommended' by me!"

Heather R. Huhman
Founder & President: Come Recommended, ComeRecommended.com HeatherHuhman.com, Author of Books: "#ENTRYLEVELtweet: Taking Your Career from Classroom to Cubicle" and "Lies, Damned Lies & Internships: The Truth About Getting from Classroom to Cubicle"

"Lisa needs to teach this material to college students! I'm a student who will be graduating soon and found her book super helpful with not only preparing for job interviews, but for insights on how to prepare myself for entering the 'real world' workforce. I'll now be going in with the right mindset, focused on my Personal Brand, from Day One!"

Maggy Perez
College Senior, Major: Graphic Design

"I'm a 60-something retired business professional and, for a variety of reasons, I have decided to come out of retirement and re-enter the workforce part-time. Lisa's book was extremely helpful in helping me determine 'who' I am at this new stage of my life as well as 'what' type of career I want to pursue. I'm now very clear on the answers to both of those questions which I know will make my job search and interviews more successful. Initially I was apprehensive about coming out of retirement but now I'm excited about the possibilities ahead of me!"

Thom Pemberton
Author of: "More of a Blessing than a Curse: Surviving Pancreatic Cancer" (Expected Release: 2014)

"This book was so helpful! I only wish something like this was written when I first entered the professional workforce 25 years ago! It would have made my career journey a lot easier. But even as a seasoned 50 year-old female executive it has provided me with tools and ideas that have been extremely useful in my career growth now. Thank you, Lisa!"

Cathy F.
Finance Manager @ Fortune 1000 Company, (Telecommunications)

"I recently accepted a new position within my company and this move got me really thinking more about my career path and future. So when I came across Lisa's book the timing was perfect! Even though I have been in the workforce for 15 years, it seriously helped me focus on my leadership style and the professional image I want moving forward. I also thought the Personal Branding exercises that are included were not only easy to follow but very interesting to do. Honestly, I think this book should be required reading for everyone that has the passion to succeed!"

Krista L.
Director of Social Media, Consumer Electronics Technology Company,
San Jose, CA

"I'm a Millennial who has been in the workforce for five years and Lisa's book has been invaluable on many levels. I now focus on my Personal Branding every day and it has truly helped me determine how I want to be known at work, as well as where I want to go with my career. This should be recommended reading for all employees!"

Jennifer L.
Sales Rep @ Fortune 500 Company (Medical Industry)

"I attended Lisa's 'Personal Branding for Career Success' workshop and it was life changing! I'm 48 and started to feel like I'd hit a wall in my career so attending her workshop, and then reading her book, really gave me helpful tools to get out of my rut. I can honestly say that her expertise, insights and strategies have made a big difference in how well things are going for me professionally now."

Dave D.
Sr. Director of Channel Marketing (Software Industry)

INTRODUCTION

Why Care About Developing a Personal Leadership Brand?

Hello! And welcome to my fourth business book. I was prompted to write this book based on countless people from many different companies, at all different career levels, constantly asking me if I could recommend a good book on how to develop a unique Personal Brand at work.

Most "branding" books are written about company or product branding, or for self-employed people, however there are *very few written for employees* who want to stand out at work (and/or in their industry) to achieve career success. So I felt this was an important topic to tackle and I see the interest in this topic growing daily.

Now, you may think that developing a Personal Leadership Brand seems silly. Well, I'm here to tell you that it is anything but "silly". I am hired by major, well-known corporations to conduct workshops for a wide variety of their employee groups on how and why to develop a Personal Leadership Brand. And, even though attendance to my workshops is often based on a voluntary basis (versus a boss saying they *have to attend*), they always attract capacity crowds.

So, it's not just me *saying* this is important…the attendance numbers I experience prove that smart employees *know* it's an important component of reaching their personal career goals, and *their employers* know it, too. Plus, at every workshop I conduct, I get a lot of employees who are 40+ years-old coming up to me afterwards saying they wish they'd known more about Personal Branding when they were younger because it would have gotten them farther in their careers, faster.

But why is there so much interest in Personal Leadership Branding nowadays? Because the workforce is more competitive! And I don't mean just for getting a job, I also mean for moving up the ladder if you're already employed.

In addition to wanting more notoriety at work, many people who attend my workshops also want to achieve more notoriety within their industry. Sure, they want success in the workplace, but they also want to be a *big fish outside of the office.* They want to be asked to speak at industry tradeshows and conventions, and they want industry media to contact them for interviews. Why? Many employees want to be positioned as Thought Leaders (aka: celebrities) within their industry; not just be "known" where they work. And, quite honestly, that's very smart, but we'll discuss that later in this book.

So...what is Personal Branding? Short answer: A strong Personal Leadership Brand allows all that's strong and effective about your personal and professional style to become known (in a deliberate and managed way) to your colleagues up, down, and across the organization, thus enabling you to generate maximum value and unique "distinction" for yourself.

However, while every employee has some sort of Personal Brand (that was either created *by* them knowingly or created *for* them *un*knowingly), few methodologies exist to help employees brand and promote 'them' strategically.

And, as with product or company branding, if you do not take control of developing, establishing, and managing your (personal) brand, and actually put some thought into it versus just letting it happen organically, other people will do it for you... and it may not always be accurate or personally favorable.

This is why many successful executives put time and effort into developing their Personal Leadership Brand and letting it be known. The good news is that regardless of your age or status in the workforce, it's never too late, or too early, to start developing and managing your Personal Leadership Brand —because there's no downside in doing it!

Therefore, I don't care if you're 18 years-old or 65+. The time to start focusing on YOU is now. So let's get started!

Lisa Was Recently Voted One of the "Top 30 Most Influential Brand Gurus in the World" by Over 22,000 Industry Professionals!

Lisa Orrell, CPC
The Generations Relations & Leadership Expert
SPEAKER • TRAINER • CERTIFIED LEADERSHIP COACH
AUTHOR • THOUGHT LEADER

Lisa@TheOrrellGroup.com
1-888-254-LISA
www.TheOrrellGroup.com

Join Lisa Online:
Twitter @GenerationsGuru • Facebook • LinkedIn • YouTube

PART ONE

Start by Understanding Who You Are... and Aren't!

"Outstanding leaders go out of the way to boost the self-esteem of their personnel. If people believe in themselves, it's amazing what they can accomplish."

Sam Walton
Founder of Wal-Mart (opened his first store in 1962)

"Be aware that people are watching what you say and what you don't say, and what you do and don't do. Your next career opportunities, and indeed reputation (Personal Brand), will be impacted by the actions and decisions you make day-to-day, every day."

(Female) Senior Vice President
Fortune 500 Company

INTRODUCTION TO PART ONE

It never fails to surprise me the response I get when I ask this question at the beginning of the Personal Branding Workshops I conduct for employee groups: "By a show of hands, how many of you are in a leadership role at this company?"

Out of an audience size of 30-500 people, ranging in age and experience level, maybe 5% of the attendees will raise their hands. So I ask it AGAIN to make the point that *everyone* in that venue should be raising a hand! Why? Because it doesn't matter what title or role the company has given you. Every employee should be in a leadership mindset because the sooner you are the sooner you start *conducting yourself like one*. And THAT impacts your Personal Brand.

Therefore, Part One of this book is comprised of eight chapters intended to provide you with principles, tips and strategies on how to be an effective and influential leader in the workforce. There are many people, possibly more experienced than you, who still don't have a grip on their leadership style (and don't even think about it), and their Personal Brands suffer because of it. How do I know? I am hired to coach them one-on-one...so they don't lose their jobs.

It truly amazes me how many people don't take the time to improve their leadership skills or really look at "who they are", yet wonder why they have on-going employee or co-worker issues, suffer from turnover in their department, and never feel as though people respect them at work. And what's the root cause of this? Themselves! They don't take responsibility for their actions, and continue to think everyone else has a problem.

I don't want that to be *you*. The sooner you can start to learn about "true" leadership, begin to hone your personal style, and understand how this all maps to developing your Personal Leadership Brand, the better off you'll be. Plus, the better off everyone around you will be! And I don't care whether you are currently working in the mailroom or as a receptionist, or in a high profile management role, or even still in school; developing your leadership mindset needs to start now!

So if you're aspiring to be more than just a cog-in-the-wheel at work or in your industry, keep reading. People with strong leadership skills and a leadership mindset stand out and make a difference…and that impacts their Personal Brand at work.

I will warn you that some of what you'll read in this section may seem a bit like "psycho-babble", but it is all about *the mind*; your mind! As you read this section, take time for self-reflection. Ask yourself things like: Do I currently do that? Do I handle situations like that? Can I improve my way of doing this? Will that tip or principle benefit me? How can I apply this info to improve myself OR to become the person I *aspire* to be?

This really is all about you. So don't just *read* the information; *internalize* the information and learn from it! And, remember, none of this will help you, in any way, if you don't *take action* on it. That's like reading a weight loss book but then never actually trying the diet and fitness plan outlined in it…then complaining to everyone that your clothes are still too tight.

Okay, I'll get off my soapbox…let's jump into Part One!

CHAPTER ONE

The Definition of a Leader & How to Think Like One

What is a leader? Are they born or made? Is a leader someone with the right genetics for the role or are the skills to motivate, inspire, and engage something that can be learned?

The term "a natural leader" is applied to many successful business people...but what does it mean exactly?

Sure, some natural leaders are born that way. A quick visit to a nearby sandbox can provide an eye-opening education. Even at the tender age of three or four, instinctive leadership abilities are demonstrated as one child wrangles the others into group play, divides the assets (like shovels), and keeps the play area humming along nicely building an integrated series of sand piles, roads, etc.

There is certainly dramatic evidence about innate leadership abilities. However, there is equally dramatic evidence that the skill-set required to lead is one that *can be learned and mastered by anyone*...even someone who has never shown any signs of leadership traits.

Fake It Until You Make It...But That Gets You Only So Far!

Many see a leader as the person who *takes charge.* This leads to the discovery of a psychology tool used by leaders in business, politics, and every imaginable arena of human pursuit: the power of perception. If you want to be perceived as a leader or effective team player at work, act like one. Leaders speak authoritatively, even when they may feel tentative. Leaders offer ideas even when they're not certain others will approve.

But does the person who takes charge always deserve the power? Nope. Unfortunately, people who possess the outward attributes of leadership – a powerful presence, a strong verbal style, etc. – may not really have what it takes on the inside. So while it is important to act like a leader so that people will perceive you as such, it's equally important that you don't fake your way up the ladder with a hollow leadership façade that you won't be able to maintain. Trust me, it won't take long for those around you to know you're faking it…and that's when the backlash begins, and your Personal Brand becomes diluted.

That is why it's so important to get past posing as a leader, or simply thinking you're a great employee, and start truly being one. Using a loud voice, bossing people around, forcing your ideas on people, not listening to others, only (really) caring about yourself, and being caught up in your title or position, are all *respect killers*. They may move you up, or have you moved you, the ladder the a few times, *but they won't keep you moving up it*. It's typically the employees with a more respected Personal Leadership Brand that will land the prime promotions.

Quite honestly, if the negative traits I just listed sound like you, it's time for an attitude adjustment. As you continue to read this chapter and book, you'll quickly see that effective and respected leaders are totally the opposite of what I just described.

Defining Terms

In order to become a leader, it's important to first define the goal. So, *what is a leader?* The answer is complex and, more importantly, evolutionary. The skills and attributes that defined a business leader during the Industrial Revolution are certainly different than those defining a captain of industry in the Computer Age. Or are they?

In truth, the single most important defining characteristic of leadership is actually quite constant: A leader is someone whose knowledge (competence), moral compass (character), and personal performance values (ethics), underline trust in others. To achieve that end, you must first trust (and respect) yourself. But I'm not talking about having a big ego; most people with big egos are really insecure and not driven by a very strong moral compass, and often don't care about others. And, more importantly, they may be the leader but they're not necessarily a *respected* leader.

Six Steps to Thinking Like a Leader

We've all heard the phrase "You are what you eat", but it is really more accurate to say, "You are what you think." How you receive, process, and respond in your head to what's going on around you will determine how you act in reality. But more than anything, thoughts influence how you act, react, look, and sound in any given situation, especially in a leadership role.

Self-image comes from within...from your thoughts. So does self-confidence. These two key leadership attributes are things we create for ourselves by learning to control our thoughts. You may have heard the term *Reactive Mind*, coined by L. Ron Hubbard, the founder of Dianetics. Hubbard claimed that the Reactive Mind *stores impressions of past events, which occurred while the person was unconscious or otherwise not completely aware.*

I'm not a Hubbard groupie at all, but I do like this little nugget from his philosophy. It's the idea that we frequently *react without thinking, and often inappropriately.* Rather than respond to the current "real" situation we're in, our reactive minds make a *habitual response.* This knee-jerk reaction is influenced more by something that happened in the past rather than what is happening in the present.

At first glance, it would seem that choosing a response based on experience makes sense. It's the essence of learning. A child who is accidentally burned learns to stay away from fire. That's good. The problem arises when that child continues to avoid fire in even a controlled and safe situation – say the candles on a birthday cake. *The response is not appropriate to the situation, even though it may feel right.*

Thoughts that <u>factor in</u> past experience, without assessing the real-time facts are counter-productive. Unfortunately, these hot-wired thoughts are frequently centered on negative self-image and undermine self-confidence. It's unfortunate because how you see yourself will influence how others see you and respond to you.

Here's the bottom line: It is impossible to be an effective leader of others, or a team player, when you are stuck in the past mentally and feel haunted by failure. Leadership is all about image and how others perceive you, but you can't fake it! It is the natural outgrowth of the positive self-image that you have created on the inside, not an artificial persona that you put on like a raincoat. If you want others to believe in your competence, you must exude a true inner self-confidence that gives them a reason to do so.

With the right thoughts as your foundation, there's nothing you can't accomplish. The goal then is to take affirmative action to control your mind and turn it into a reliable support system. "But how?" you may be wondering.

The first step is to take an inventory of your thoughts and see what your mind is manufacturing each day. Do you think I'm kidding? Not at all! I often require my coaching clients to do this and it's very helpful. If you can't start to control your mind, versus letting it control you, you won't start to see patterns and start to really "know you". And if you think this seems like a waste of time, think again. Some of the most well-known and respected leaders I know have done this, and continue to do this. It gives them clarity, keeps them grounded and in-tuned with themselves, and that enables them to lead effectively.

So, here's the deal, the same way that a dieter keeps a food journal to gain insights into their eating patterns you should consider keeping a **Thought Journal**. In your "mental diary", which can be a handwritten paper journal, Word doc, or a private blog (that others can't access), focus on these questions daily:

- What's going on inside your head?
- What things are on your mind throughout the day?
- Are your thoughts generally positive or negative?

You may have a general impression of your mindset, but you'll never know what's *really* happening until you have written down your thoughts and examined them. You may be shocked at how often you're shooting yourself in the foot with a self-negating thought!

Now comes the interesting part. At the end of the day, look at each negative thought and work to reframe it into something positive. This isn't as hard as it may appear.

For example:
- Negative Thought: I can't believe I have to attend that training workshop!
- Re-framed: Training workshops help me become more proficient at my job, and that makes me more valuable, so I *want* to go!

This isn't "happy talk" or lying to yourself. It is merely putting a more positive, a more *hopeful*, spin on the situation. By recognizing that you are becoming *more* proficient, you are opening the door to the fact that you will one day achieve mastery. Remember, you're never too old to learn and you'll never know everything.

Key point: Hope and optimism are vital to leaders. Hope and optimism help keep them focused on possibilities that can prevent them from becoming mired in any immediate crisis. Your mind can be a breeding ground for toxic negativity, or it can be fertile soil where positive solutions grow. Basically, the mindset you choose becomes the foundation for, and affects every aspect of, your Personal Brand.

Here are the *Six Steps to Thinking Like a Leader:*

Step 1: Take Charge: Thoughts are powerful, but you can keep them from running amok inside your head and influencing your behavior. Make a commitment to control what you think about. This means making a *daily effort* to consciously program positive thoughts or affirmations into your mind.

Step 2: Watch Your Language: Would you talk to other people the way you talk to yourself in your head? You probably wouldn't dare! Use the word "should" as infrequently as possible. Treat yourself with the same respect and dignity you'd treat anyone else in your life...but that doesn't mean you should give yourself a free ride.

For example, instead of thinking, 'I'm bad about not holding staff meetings consistently,' reframe the thought as, 'I will schedule staff meetings every Monday at 9:30 am, and that will start next week.' That way you're *talking* action and that means you're more likely to *take* action.

Step 3: Remember the Good Times: One of the most insidious thoughts that invade a leader's mind is, "What if?" The more creative you are, the more terrifying these worst-case scenarios will be, as you imagine computer network failures, supply chain disasters, personnel flare-ups, and other situations that could overwhelm you. You can't see into your future, and that's scary.

But here's a suggestion: Empower yourself with real memories of the past and all the things you've achieved. Make a list of all the obstacles you've hurdled in the past and the tough situations where you've come out on top. This will be your go-to mental "safe place". It's where you should turn your thoughts whenever you start to doubt your capabilities to remind yourself that you have successfully handled challenges and obstacles before.

As a leader at any level, you will always be faced with challenges that seem unbelievable. And, as with most people, you'll get scared and wonder how the heck you're going to handle the situation. This is where having the "safe place" comes in very handy. Also, you may often find yourself feeling alone and having to boost yourself up. It is critical to your success to be able to *empower yourself* during those challenging times.

Step 4: Let Go: When a difficult situation arises, do you deal with things coolly on the outside, but spend the rest of the day raging on the inside? The fact that you were able to mask your emotions may seem positive, but it's not really. It's exhausting to be "angry on the inside". Harboring resentment is a huge drain that zaps your mental, emotional, and even your physical reserves. It's also pointless.

Unless you can take action to rectify a situation, there is no point in thinking about it. It doesn't matter who was right and who was wrong. What matters is what you can learn from it and how you can use what you've learned in the future. Beyond that, what's past is past.

I realize that "letting go" is often easier said than done, so here are some tools to consider: If the issue is with a person, it's important for you to speak with them quickly, in a calm and private setting. And if it's a significant issue you want to discuss with this individual, such as bullying or sexual harassment, make sure your Manager is present. Large or small, you have to discuss the issue in order to move on.

Another tool to consider is simply writing your feelings and thoughts down. There's a reason many people keep journals! Journals help them express their feelings, *process* what they're feeling and thinking, and oftentimes enables them to "let go" so they can move on.

Step 5: Set a "Mental" Training Schedule: Unused thought patterns, like unused muscles, can get creaky and out of shape. The best way to avoid mental atrophy is with regularly scheduled "workouts" throughout the day. Block out time each day to focus on the process of *right thinking* and <u>define a specific action you can take</u>.

Let's say you have a habit of thinking, "There's too much work!" Make a deal with yourself that from 1PM until 3PM, if that thought comes into your mind, you'll immediately switch your mindset and think to yourself, "I, along with my team, am working hard to meet the deadline and we will make it." Before long, you'll create a habit and your mind will automatically make the switchover to positive thoughts without any conscious help from you.

Step 6: Acknowledge Progress: Perfection is a process and a goal, not a destination, when it comes to managing your thoughts. The real measure of success in this area is ongoing progress. Remember to acknowledge where you've been so that you can appreciate how far you've come instead of worrying about how far you have to go. With your Thought Journal, it will be easy to monitor and mark the genuine progress you're making.

A good way to re-enforce any positive effort – in this case a positive thought – is with a **tangible reward**. If your Thought Journal reveals that you've gone 24 hours without a self-negating thought...or 3 days without holding on to anger...or haven't beaten yourself up with "shoulda-woulda-coulda" for a week...treat yourself to an extra latte or a massage (or whatever you consider a reward). This way, you'll begin to unconsciously <u>associate your positive thoughts with positive experiences.</u>

Lisa's Closing Comments:

I told you this chapter may sound a bit like "psycho-babble", but it's important psychobabble. I'm not just blowing smoke up your skirt (or pant leg). You can read a million books on leadership that provide general tips and principles on *how to lead others*. But if you don't really get to know yourself, and be honest with yourself about the self-sabotage dialogue that runs your mind, you'll struggle with *leading yourself* and your Personal Brand will suffer!

I want you to be a respected leader, not a feared leader (there's a difference). Feared leaders suffer a lot (unnecessarily). They don't trust or truly believe in themselves, they don't trust their team members, they live in a paranoid state, everyone is nice or respectful to their face but not behind their backs, their team members are rarely loyal, they have trouble attracting and retaining good employees, and they just tend to have a constant negativity "cloud" around them.

But truly respected leaders tend to experience the total opposite. Sure, they face major challenges, any leader does. But they don't get bogged down, and have all their energy zapped, with all the other crud I listed.

Keeping a Thought Journal is a great way to begin to see the thoughts that can negatively impact your career journey, so I hope you'll consider trying it! Even just for a week.

Another interesting exercise to keep yourself in a positive frame of mind is the following (and it's another thing I encourage my coaching clients to do): Each night before you fall asleep, take a few minutes to write down, or mentally list, 4-5 things that <u>acknowledge</u> something positive about yourself. This can be "general" or something tangible (like a task you accomplished that day), that is about you.

And each morning, while showering, driving to work, or whatever, list 4-5 things you have <u>gratitude</u> for. This list is meant to be about things "external": family, friends, co-workers, your neighbor, your dog, your house, your partner, etc.

If doing this is of interest to you, here's a cool mobile app to consider: *Gratitude Journal* by HappyTapper™. It's hugely popular and worth checking out!

Focusing on acknowledging yourself, and focusing on gratitude, are great ways to start and end each day. Plus, they are effective tools for keeping you grounded and elevating your (positive) leadership mindset…thus positively affecting your Personal Leadership Brand!

CHAPTER TWO

Manager Mindset vs. Leadership Mindset

The confusion between the role of a manager and a leader has tripped up more than one business professional and cost many companies their very existence. Is 'the person in charge' automatically a leader? If you're managing other people, are you also leading them, by default? Just what is the difference between the two?

According to the current wisdom, managers are principally administrators; they write business plans, set budgets, monitor progress, and, yes, they manage people (but sometimes without the concept of an effective leadership mindset).

Leaders, on the other hand, get organizations and people to change. Most business executives and owners have a mix of management and leadership skills. And, quite often, both skill sets are necessary to run a successful business and team.

But typically, only the top executives can set direction in a company. Setting direction is different from setting goals. A goal is concrete and measurable: "We must sell ten widgets by next Tuesday." Direction is broader. Leaders set direction with a vision, a mission, and operating principles that embody the company's direction and values.

Here is a key point that can settle confusion for you: Even if you just manage one person, regardless of what your role/title is, you are also a leader. Yes, you may be considered an entry-level employee or a "manager or supervisor" on paper, but you are leading, too. Even though your current position may not be one that "sets direction for the entire company", you are still a leader. For example, you may not be responsible for managing one person at work on a daily basis, however you can find yourself in *sporadic* leadership roles where you do manage people, like: volunteering to coordinate an event for your department or taking the lead on a new project.

So whether you are actually in a true management role with

employees, or assuming a short-term leadership role for your group, cultivating a leadership mindset is critical.

Everyone from the CEO to an entry-level Sales Manager is in a *management* role (managing other people). But successful managers are also successful leaders, and successful leaders stand out and move up!

Therefore, don't think "leadership" is something that only occurs once you're in an executive role. Your leadership mindset needs to start right now...regardless of your current role or experience-level. Again, getting yourself into a *leadership mindset* is the foundation of developing and managing your Personal Brand.

Defining Terms

A manger is a person that achieves company objectives through the actions and efforts of subordinates. A manager provides feedback to staff and serves as a liaison between executives and employees. A manager controls resources and expenditures, but his/her powers are defined by the organizational structure, which also defines the amount of influence managers have over subordinates.

A leader is the person that **sets company objectives and makes decisions** that other people follow; someone that guides or inspires others. Leaders apply the same practices that good managers use. However, unlike managers who provide feedback, leaders solicit it. Leaders listen to what their subordinates say and take the time to explore underlying issues. They help employees solve their own problems by *providing an environment where people know they are accepted.*

Both a manager and a leader may know a business reasonably well, but the leader must know the business to a finer degree and from a different viewpoint. Leaders must grasp the underlying market forces that determine the past and present trends in the business's niche so they can generate a vision and strategy to bring about its future development and growth.

A crucial sign of a good leader is **an honest attitude towards the facts** and objective truths. Conversely, a subjective leader obscures the facts for the sake of narrow self-interest, partisan interest, or prejudice. *Many managers sometimes fall into the trap of subjective leadership.* They become more intent on sending good news to the executive office to ensure their own professional health and longevity than to honestly deliver the bad news that could and should be a catalyst for needed change.

We all know that rotten managers and co-workers have been the focus of jokes forever in TV, movies, comic strips, etc. Even worse, they have been the focus of jokes in reality, too. Do you really want to be one of *those* employees?

Reality check: If whenever you walk into a group of your employees or co-workers and everyone stops talking, you probably are. If your employees or co-workers don't have much to say to you, you probably are. If your team always seems to have low morale and enthusiasm, except the week before you go on vacation, you probably are. And if you're a manager whose employees quit a lot, you probably are.

If any of this remotely describes what you experience at work, I'm glad you are reading this book. **It means your Personal Brand needs an overhaul!**

Good leaders make people want to achieve their very best, rather than just meeting a day-to-day objective. Leaders with a knack for setting realistic goals, and who provide guidance and feedback to empower others, gain **the respect and support** of their staff. Period.

The Trust Factor

Perhaps most importantly, the trust a leader demonstrates <u>in</u> his/her staff builds the employees' motivation and commitment. And a leader that is honorable and trustworthy will always focus on *doing the right thing*, and their staff will willingly follow them anywhere!

Basically, the ability to influence comes from trust. But maximum–influence only accrues to those leaders who possess and demonstrate these three characteristics consistently: personal expertise, integrity, and empathy. Do you?

Management consists primarily of three things: analysis, problem solving, and planning. If you go to any management course it'll probably be composed of those three elements. But leadership consists of vision and values and the communication of those things. That ability to *create a vision* is another main difference between leadership and management.

The Good Book (aka: Bible) says, "Without a vision the people perish." And any good *business* bible will tell you that when a leader has no vision, companies perish, too!

It is tempting to see managers as drudges who feed the machine while leaders create visions of a better world. Some business experts criticize those who denigrate managers in order to elevate leaders, and praise managers for bringing order, stability, and predictability to the workplace. I totally agree with this. However, I just wish more managers would take on "leadership" traits when it comes to how they manage their employees.

I realize not every person in a company wants to be a senior executive or "lead" the whole business. But to not embrace some fundamental, effective leadership qualities within your management style that will make your team happier and more productive is BEING LAZY!

Have you ever heard this saying: "People don't leave companies; they leave managers (or co-workers)"? It has been around forever and there is a reason…it's true! Think about it. Aside from a major change in their circumstances, like needing to move far away, having a baby, needing to care for a loved one full time, or getting an absolutely amazing job offer, *an employee normally leaves a job because of a person they work with or work for.*

23 Key Differences between a Manager Mindset & Leadership Mindset:

The following list provides **23 Core Competencies** that define key differences between leaders and managers. And, as you'll see, leadership skills tend to be *flexible, responsive to change, and future-oriented.*

1. Leaders set a standard of excellence – Managers set a standard for performance

2. Leaders are policy-makers – Managers set standard operating procedures

3. Leaders seek employee commitment – Managers seek employee compliance

4. Leaders are proactive – Managers are reactive

5. Leaders create change – Managers maintain the status quo

6. Leaders take risk – Managers are risk-averse

7. Leaders are analytical decision-makers – Managers are intuitive decision-makers

8. Leaders value planning – Managers value action

9. Leaders are passionate – Managers are controlling

10. Leaders can lead people – Managers manage work

11. Leaders originate – Managers imitate

12. Leaders can create followers – Managers have subordinates

13. Leaders can think long-term – Managers think short-term

14. Leaders can set the direction – Managers plan the route

15. Leaders persuade – Managers supervise

16. Leaders develop strategies – Managers develop tactics

17. Leaders can make decisions – Managers implement policy

18. Leaders use personal charisma – Managers rely on bestowed authority

19. Leaders have a transformational style – Managers have a transactional style

20. Leaders make and break the rules – Managers implement the rules

21. Leaders are pathfinders – Mangers use old roads

22. Leaders give credit – Managers assign blame

23. Leaders care about what's right – Managers care about being right

Lisa's Closing Comments:

I'll keep this short. Managers that don't choose to embody important leadership qualities, suffer. And their employees and companies suffer. Shortsighted employees and managers tend to focus on process, procedures, and themselves, *and not focus on other people.* Leaders focus on the latter, first. Be a manager or employee who blends management skills with effective leadership qualities, and you will succeed in any role at any level your career path takes you…and this will become a key, respected component of your Personal Leadership Brand.

Now, let's talk about seven Ironclad Attributes of an Exceptional Leader!

CHAPTER THREE
Attributes of an Exceptional Leader

We all know much has been written on the subject of leadership and many business writers and motivational speakers have codified the attributes they believe are essential for leaders. Frequently, however, their descriptions focus upon traits that make a leader <u>personable, affable, and well liked.</u> It's nice to be liked, but Leadership is not (just) a popularity contest. As a leader, in a long term or short-term role, you will be faced with making decisions that won't make everyone happy. And that's okay. As long as your employees or your co-workers respect you and trust you, the ones who were not happy with your decisions will (normally) get over it. And being clear about your Personal Brand develops respect and trust!

We live in an era plagued by cynicism and doubt, especially in regards to leaders and their motives, not only in corporate, but also government. This creates a special challenge for people in leadership roles today who need to be trusted and respected in order to achieve the kind of 'popularity' that will enable them to achieve success, as well.

• **When the leader is respected,** which means they are at the very least trusted and probably liked as well, then this enables the leader to make proposals that followers will take seriously.

• **If the respect for the leader is strong,** then the followers will likely accept the solution being offered, even if they are not that convinced by the arguments that the leader is putting forward.

• **If the leader is <u>not</u> respected,** then people will follow them only if they see no other viable choice. But people will also (eventually) leave and seek a leader they do respect.

Someone Has to Follow the Leader

Almost everyone can describe the characteristics of an exceptional leader. Their descriptions may be based on a single great boss or on a collage of desirable features that they recognized in several leaders, but most people seem to have some idea of what's essential. But whatever else might be true about the role, you're not a good "leader" unless you have followers who respect you.

Leadership and management are often used in the same breath, largely because those who are appointed managers seek also to be leaders. I mentioned this in the previous chapter, but to recap (briefly), here are two key points:

• Managers have subordinates who obey commands in a basic transaction of <u>obedience in return for pay and conditions.</u> But when working for a manager without strong leadership qualities, who you don't respect, you (as an employee) are probably on the lookout for another job, right?

• Good leaders, however, have <u>followers who choose to follow</u> them. And good leaders often have followers who are happy to be working for them, and compensation isn't their number one priority. They may even get job offers for more pay, but they just really like their boss and don't want to risk getting a new one that makes their lives miserable. And, yes, a bad boss makes your life miserable, so don't be one.

Role Reversal

The role of leader has many facets. Good leaders pay close attention to followers to ensure their ongoing motivation. If followers' buy-in decreases, then the leader must act to re-motivate them. This creates a leader-follower inversion, in which <u>the leader becomes the follower and vice versa.</u>

In this way, the roles of leader and follower are fluid. There is a constant shift of influence and motivation. A good leader, however, doesn't let the employees ultimately run the show. He/she always remains at the helm.

Pied Piper Power Play

A leader's *power* is not inherently good or bad, but just part of the equation. The **power dynamic** exists in leadership relationships because leadership is a process of influence, and <u>power provides influence potential</u>.

A leader's potential to influence others, to give them a reason to follow, flows from the leader's base of power. When used correctly, that power enables leaders to influence because the leader is *trusted, revered and/or considered an expert.*

An interesting comment on this comes from the arena...not the business arena, but the sports arena. Legendary NFL Quarterback, Joe Namath, said, *"To be a leader, you have to make people want to follow you, and nobody wants to follow someone who doesn't know where he is going."*

What do successful leaders do to become effective Pied Pipers? What separates a leader from being a *basic* manager? And why do so many managers fail to live up to their leadership potential? The answer can be found, in part, in the attributes below.

Seven Ironclad Attributes of an Exceptional Leader:

The following seven attributes are reflections of character and personal integrity. They must be developed through self-discipline, time and pressure. They are not inherited and cannot not be "faked" successfully...at least not for long.

Attribute #1: Sets High Standards: Leaders set high standards for their followers...and themselves. Successful leaders are consistent in demanding of themselves compliance with the standards that they espouse. Those who do not are only fooling themselves.

Attribute #2: Lives Up to Those Standards: Leaders live up to the standards they have set. Nothing disqualifies a would-be leader faster than a **double standard**, one for them and another for those under their authority. Subordinates will quickly see through the duplicity, and disgust, grudging obedience, and resignation letters will rapidly replace loyalty.

Attribute #3: Mentors Those Who Follow: We all need guidance. However many mediocre leaders expect their followers to attain the standards set by their leadership without ever teaching them exactly how. Effective leaders, on the other hand, *invest themselves in their followers.* They make a concerted effort to communicate verbally not only <u>what is expected, but also how to achieve it.</u>

Attribute #4: Creates and Shares a Vision: Effective leaders are driven by a singular vision not of what is, but of what will be. And they make sure that everyone around them understands and buys into that vision of *where the organization (and/or department) is going and what is necessary to attain that goal.* A splintered vision, or one that is implemented in a fragmented manner, will always result in **competing interests** within the organization, vying for resources, and each person thinking their particular function and sphere of effort is most important. This is when employee morale takes a plunge.

Attribute #5: Makes the Hard Choices When Necessary: Effective leaders are characterized by a willingness to make the hard decisions when necessary...and sometimes under extreme pressure. Yet it is human nature that in the face of crisis, stall...keep all the options open. True leaders, however, don't stall. They assess and execute. They know that stalling, or going into a state of denial, just makes things worse.

Attribute #6: Is Visible: Nowadays a department or company can have employees spread out all over the globe, thus requiring a lot of virtual communication. If this describes your company, do customers and staff alike have a clear and constant sense that someone, a real person, is really in charge of the group or project? This is something I see companies and managers struggle with a lot.

As the manager of a virtual group, you have GOT to conduct weekly group calls or video conferences with your team, and also communicate with each remote team member one-on-one regularly. Employees in this type of structure complain to me all the time that their boss hardly ever speaks to them one-on-one, and that can make a virtual employee feel out of touch.

To command respect, which is a key component of trust, *and in turn the essential ingredient for creating followers*, leaders must be highly visible!

Heck, I know many mid-level managers who <u>don't</u> have virtual teams and stay hidden in their offices…rarely meeting or speaking with employees, avoiding customers (thinking their sales reps can handle them), and basically avoiding anything that remotely looks like a "leadership" quality. Don't let that be you.

Attribute #7: Instills Hope in Those Who Follow: The final attribute of successful leaders is their ability to instill hope. None of us can continue to grow, develop and perform at our highest potential without hope. Hope for success, hope for recognition and reward, and most importantly, hope that indeed we can make a difference in the long-term outcome. Hope supplies the essential fuel that enables the human spirit to continue moving forward, especially in the face of severe adversity. So strive to be a leader who instills hope in your team, as a group and as individuals. Because even though this book is all *about you*, it's ultimately *for them, too.*

Lisa's Closing Comments:

Sure, the title on your business card and your role within your company will oftentimes come with inherent respect. But it stops there. If you don't possess the attributes of a good leader, and work at becoming an effective one on an on-going basis, the title on your card won't matter. Your co-workers, employees, and supervisors will lose respect for you, and trust will disappear. And your Personal Brand will be (potentially) tarnished at your company forever.

The only person who can create, build and maintain your brand as an effective, respected employee, is you.

I talk to tons of employees, privately or in my workshops,

that openly share frustrations about certain co-workers or their bosses. The complaints include things like my boss: thinks s/he knows everything; disregards other peoples' opinions; rarely asks for input from our team; communicates in a condescending way;or has a big ego. I'm not kidding when I say that some of my workshops often turn into group therapy sessions!

And I know many of *you* share those same gripes about your boss and/or specific co-workers. But why should you be one of *the people griped about*? Why not work on your personal leadership style to only encompass traits that make you respected, well liked, and effective? Seriously...why wouldn't you want a Personal Brand like THAT?

The old school of traditional management and leadership styles has created a workforce where 60% of employees are dissatisfied and disengaged. I challenge you to help reduce that awful statistic! The attributes and principles in this book are best practices that the most effective leaders in our history, and those currently employed, possess.

This isn't rocket science; it's common sense! The time to change the "negative" attitudes in the workforce is now, and that comes from good leadership. So I beg you to lead the charge by focusing on creating your own, unique, *positive* Personal Leadership Brand, and then pay it forward by helping others do it, too!

CHAPTER FOUR
Communication Strategies for Effective Leadership

Within organizations there are many channels of communication that allow for an ongoing exchange of information: downward, upward, horizontal and informal.

Downward communications from supervisors to employees tends to flow in one direction, often discouraging response, whereas information sent **upward** from subordinates to superiors encourages feedback. Sharing information **horizontally** across department lines or among peers can help eliminate duplication and improve teamwork.

Meanwhile, the informal communication channel, the social interaction among associates known as "the grapevine", can be the most influential in business.

At the center of all this information flow is the leader who understands that all *channels of communication are intrinsic to organizational performance*. But navigating the communication "waters" can be challenging for people of any age in a leadership role; which is why there are many managers/supervisors who don't tend to do a great job when it comes to communicating with their team members and co-workers.

In this chapter, we'll not only cover ways that you can effectively communicate in "general" terms with your team (as a whole) regarding broad company decisions and initiatives, but also strategies to help you communicate with your employees and co-workers one-on-one.

I will tell you right now that being known as an exceptional communicator, regardless of your current level or position, is a Personal Brand attribute highly successful people focus on!

Mum's the Word

Decision-makers are often admonished to include people in the decision-making process because it enhances the likelihood of acceptance. But this is not always possible. As a leader, there will be times when you are involved in discussions with your superiors regarding issues that are often deep, nuanced and sometimes contentious. Simply put, the nature of the decision-making process and the features of the decision itself may make it impossible to keep your employees in the loop.

An example of this is when there is a manager's meeting where the CEO gathers you together to discuss the need to have company-wide layoffs. Or, the CEO wants to tell you the company may be acquired (or is planning to purchase another company). These can be discussions that the CEO does not want you to share with your team until further notice. Certainly, you must respect this and not let info "slip" out to your employees. This is how rumors get started, and often times it's a loose-lipped manager who gets the rumor mill moving. Don't be that person!

However the real problem arises after a confidential decision has been made. You may find that as a leader, you will be responsible for sharing the news with your team about a new company policy (the top executives may not do it). Communicating a 'done deal' decision is difficult...and leaders, fearful of having to tell their team, often give only minimal attention to doing it effectively.

The 'Hidden' Message

When we use the word *communicate*, we are referring not only to the words one uses to transfer factual information to others, but also to other unspoken "messages" that are sent and received. In a time of company or policy change, for example, an effective leader communicates the following "sub-texts" along with his/her message:

- A sense of confidence and control (or lack thereof) to employees.
- His/her own feelings about the change (within moderation and with tact).

- The degree to which he/she trusts the abilities of the employees to get through the change.
- A sense of purpose and commitment (or lack thereof).
- The degree to which he/she accepts the reactions and feelings of employees.
- Expectations regarding behavior that is seen as appropriate or inappropriate (i.e., rumor-mongering, back-room meetings, etc.).
- The degree to which he/she is connected to employees' situations and feelings, and/or is in-touch with them.

It is clear that if the leader communicates effectively, he/she will be sending messages that *decrease resistance, and encourage moving through the change* more effectively and positively. It is key, however, that although you can express empathy with your team members who express anger or confusion about the news; it is not okay for you to get on the "bashing bandwagon" along with them. Let them vent, but don't vent with them. Basically, answer any questions you've been ok'd to answer, but mainly focus on listening, being supportive, and providing encouragement.

Poor communication is repeatedly cited as a *key contributor in the failure of major change efforts*, so communication skills are increasingly regarded as a critical skill for leaders, particularly in situations where the leader is an instrumental driver of change.

Numerous studies also show that communication is closely tied to an organization's total effectiveness, which underscores why organizations need "communication champions" in order to be successful. And you, in a leadership role, will often be called upon to be one of those "champions" for sharing great company news and not so great news with your team.

When It's Not All About the Company

Now let's get into solid tips for communicating "in general" with your team members, when it has nothing to do with telling them about some big companywide initiative. This is about how you communicate, day-to-day, with your employees.

Communication itself is not a goal; it's the means to an end. Great leaders consistently strive to strengthen their interpersonal communication competencies by **building and maintaining open, supportive, and collaborative relationships** with others in the organization. In other words, communication is a two-way street with *effective* leaders participating in *dialogues* rather than *monologues*.

The essential point is that the professional world is now too complex for the leader to have all the answers. Effective leaders now realize that managing highly skilled talent in a way that gets the best out of people and benefits the company, requires them to draw solutions out of people rather than restricting themselves to just selling their own ideas and solutions. Therefore to lead effectively you need to be good at **active listening**. This means asking questions about what other people think and probing them on the pros and cons of their feedback.

Asking people for their opinions is the best way of showing that you value them which is another essential leadership trait (if you want to engage and retain key talent and/or gain respect from your co-workers).

In his book *Good to Great*, Jim Collins describes a successful leader as someone who excels at *knowing what questions to ask to draw good ideas out of their teams*. Are you good at it?

But aside from those valuable communication qualities to be aware of, let's look at these, too. Your Personal Brand *style* should incorporate ALL of them!

14 Infallible Communication Strategies for Effective Leaders:

1. Let Your Actions Speak As Loudly As Your Words: Make communications important to you personally. Take time to assess yourself on how well you communicate (up, down, around). Work on continuously improving your communication processes (written, oral, contextual, intuitive, and interpersonal).

2. Trust in Your Informal Channels: Employ an "open door" policy to gather information on what's actually happening (or not happening) in a quasi-social way. And remember that "shop talk" is an appropriate way to spend time communicating.

3. Don't Be Skimpy: When it comes to information, "too much is never enough." More communication is *always* better than less, especially during tough times when rumors may be flying around like a mosquito swarm. Plus, good communication is what *sells* changes and initiatives. And there's an additional benefit, too: Employees who feel well informed tend to be more forgiving of the occasional error.

4. Ask When Telling Doesn't Work: When employees don't understand or aren't implementing a strategy effectively, don't *tell them louder*. Repeating the same information or guessing how to clarify what they need to know is fruitless. Instead, flip your communication approach from *talk to listen,* and ask employees to talk to *you.*

5. Talk Face to Face: In-person communications play a crucial role during times of uncertainty and change. As a leader, it's vital to display a willingness to address challenging questions, listen carefully, and respond quickly to sensitive topics.

6. Is A Fact-Finder: Make regular forays to find out what's being said, heard, and what's being forwarded electronically. Make a point to give people an opportunity to be listened to. When leaders engage with their followers, they're seen as a person who *understands what's happening, who is cognizant of feelings, and who doesn't have all the answers, but who is willing to listen, learn, and take action.*

7. Don't Go With the Flow...Facilitate It: Your job in a leadership role is to ensure the <u>optimum flow of information</u> in every direction. Communicate what you know, when you know it and as often as possible (when appropriate).

8. Tells the Truth: When bad news is candidly reported, an environment is created in which <u>good news is more believable.</u>

9. Don't Just Recite the Facts, Explain Them: In business, we worship at the altar of data...raw numbers and statistics that are easy to report, but not as easy to understand. This highlights a common reason for communication disconnect. Team members don't just want a recitation from their leader, they also want an interpretation from them: "What sense do you make out of this data (aka news)? What is your conclusion? Can you share your thoughts with us?"

10. Use Emotion: Storytelling is an important tool for leaders who want to connect on an emotional level with their employees. Personal stories illustrate to followers what the leader feels and why he/she feels that way. So not only can storytelling (using your own personal stories) communicate your point(s) better, but they can *humanize* you, and build bonds with your team.

11. Communicate with Groups: Effective leaders use group communications to ensure everybody hears the news at the same time, to encourage group discussion, to generate ideas, (perhaps) start the problem-solving process, and to increase the sense of team. In something like a lay-off situation, you can call a short group meeting to announce the lay-offs in general, then immediately meet individually with each staff member to inform them of their status (if it has been determined), OR to simply provide private discussions for each person to openly communicate with you about their fears, concerns, anger, etc.

12. Communicate with Individuals: One-on-one, private communication is valuable when the information being shared is likely to cause a high degree of emotions. Individual conversations also ensure that shyer people have a chance to express themselves to you. Having regular, one-on-one meetings with each of your team members is critical.

13. Communicate Verbally When Appropriate: Oral communication provides more opportunities for getting and keeping interest and attention, to use verbal emphasis, and the chance to listen to (and remove) resistance. Verbal communications are also more likely to affect people's attitudes.

14. Communicate in Writing When Appropriate: Generally, the more emotional the issue, the more important it is to deliver the news verbally, preferably in-person. If it is information that is "light", like telling your team you want to take them to lunch next week, or that you'll be taking some vacation time next month, written is fine. For example, I know of a big company who sent out a "there will be cutbacks starting next month" mass email to all employees. Can you see what's wrong with written communication in *that* scenario?? The whole company freaked-out, had no idea about what types of "cutbacks", and they all ran to their managers (this could be you) for an explanation. Suddenly you're dealing with "angry villagers" seeking answers, and you're in total damage control mode. So, your company or boss may choose to drop news like that to the masses in writing, but whenever you have control of how information can be communicated, whether it's just to one employee, or to your whole group, be wise about how you do it.

Lisa's Closing Comments:

In my professional coach training, and in my coaching experience, I have found there are many principles of coaching those effective leaders can use, and do use, when communicating with employees. Basically, great leaders are also great coaches, even if they don't think of themselves as such.

That said, I'd like to share with you some solid communication tips pertaining to *Effective Listening & Effective Feedback* that will help you immensely...and that will impact your Personal Brand positively by being known as a great communicator:

Effective Listening:

• In the world of coaching, we're taught to listen 80% of the time and talk 20% of the time (I don't necessarily follow that ratio closely all the time, but you get the point). As a leader, that's a ratio you should also consider when meeting with an employee. You may have also heard that old saying, "You were given two ears and one mouth… use that ratio accordingly". It really boils down to another great saying, "I never learned anything while I was talking".

• Did you know that we usually only can recall about 50% of what someone said immediately after they said it? That's because very few people are good at *active listening*, and are more focused on how what the person is saying impacts *them*, and formulating their response before the person is even done talking. <u>Focus on being an active listener!</u> Be totally attentive and tuned in to the person talking, and remain "present". *Being known as a "great listener" is an extremely powerful and positive attribute for your Personal Brand.*

• Practice the use of *paraphrasing* once a person is done talking. This means responding with something like, "Just so I'm clear, what I heard you say was…" This keeps you on track, makes them feel heard and understood, and reduces the chances of miscommunication.

• Eliminate distractions! If you're communicating via phone, walk away or turn away from your computer so that you're not tempted to start checking email or work on a project. And if you're meeting with someone in your office, do NOT read email, text, IM or whatever while they are talking to you. That's rude, condescending, greatly reduces your chances of hearing them correctly, and can make the person feel totally disrespected and frustrated.

• Use the W.A.I.T. Principle: So often we interrupt people while they are talking. This happens all the time, and can be the foundation for ineffective communication and comprehension. So here's a tip to consider: Wait 10 seconds before responding to what someone just told you. This allows the person to have a few seconds to finish their thoughts and perhaps think of more things to add, and it gives you a few seconds to respond thoughtfully. Here is what the acronym W.A.I.T. stands for "**Why Am I Talking?**"

Effective Feedback: Providing good, effective feedback is often without judgment, and sometimes without your opinion (unless you are being asked your opinion).

• One tip is to ask the person *for permission* before giving the feedback. Sometimes your team member or co-worker may simply want to be venting and in a very emotional space. But you're on the verge of jumping into a whole dialogue filled with opinion and/or criticism, or you're ready to go into "fix it" mode. So you can slow them down and slow YOU down, by asking, "May I share some feedback with you?" That gives them the opportunity to say, "No, now wouldn't be good. I just wanted to vent". However if they say yes (and 99% of the time most anyone will) your "asking them permission" gives them a moment to <u>prepare for listening</u>. Be sure to try this because it works really well!

• Ask a lot of questions. Often what someone is expressing may not be the real issue or point, and you can help him or her by asking questions. Try to get past "how what they are saying makes you feel or impacts you", and focus on "them". As I mentioned before, getting good at questioning is a key trait of an effective leader.

• Try to listen to your employees or co-workers without judgment. Just because you may not relate to what they are expressing, or don't agree, doesn't mean it's wrong. Hear everyone out (employees, co-workers, your boss, etc.), because you will learn more by doing that. By not always focusing on "you", and your ideas, comments and opinions, you will be known as an effective, and respectful, leader and employee...and that's what we want for your Personal Brand!

CHAPTER FIVE

Leadership Tips for Problem Solving

Earlier in this section, leadership was defined as the ability to inspire, influence, and provide direction for people. But leadership is also a *system of approaches* to solving the problems of an organization in such a manner that the inspiration, influence, and direction come about in an effective and efficient manner.

As you read this chapter, please keep in mind that "problem solving" isn't just related to a company's challenges, but to your department's challenges and your own. The challenges you will face, or are facing, can range anywhere from to an employee who is not performing, to a process you have implemented that is not working, to goals you've established for your team that aren't being achieved.

Regardless, being known as a good problem solver for a challenge of any magnitude, is an attribute you want associated with your Personal Brand. I talk to employees all the time who complain their boss or a co-worker avoids dealing with issues. Is that a Personal Brand attribute you want to be known for? I hope not.

Rational and Appreciative Inquiry Methods for Problem Solving

There are many approaches to problem solving, and choosing the right one depends on the nature of the problem, the people involved, and the dynamics creating the problem.

The more traditional method, a *rational approach,* is typically used. It involves steps such as:

• Clarifying a description of the problem
• Analyzing causes
• Identifying alternatives
• Assessing each alternative
• Choosing an alternative

• Implementing the alternative
• Evaluating whether the problem was solved or not

Another method, that requires more personal reflection, is *appreciative inquiry.* This approach asserts that problems and solutions are often the result of <u>our own perspectives.</u> Appreciative inquiry includes:

• Identifying our best experiences in a similar situation in the past
• Thinking about what worked best then
• Envisioning the outcome after the issue has been "fixed"
• Building from our strengths to work towards the vision of the solution

Many leaders use a combination of the two methods. Appreciative inquiry can act as a "personal empowerment" approach when you are feeling overwhelmed or insecure about a challenge you're faced with. Being able to tap into past experiences you've had where you were faced with a huge obstacle, which seemed too much to handle, but successfully pulled through, is key.

In any role at work, you will face challenges, large and small, that you will be expected to handle quickly and effectively. You'll need to rely on yourself to maybe not necessarily fix everything alone, but rather empower yourself with the courage to lead the charter to solving the problem.

This is hard for many leaders…they get fearful, can't muster up courage and personal strength, and therefore "avoid" issues that often just get worse.

But once you've empowered yourself to "face" what is happening, you can use a *rational* method to create a plan for taking action.

Problem Prevention

Small problems often precede catastrophes. In fact, most large-scale failures result from a series of small errors and failures, rather than a single root cause. These small problems often cascade to create huge ones. Accident investigators in fields such as commercial aviation, the military, and medicine have shown that a chain of events and errors typically leads to a particular major disaster.

Thus, *minor failures and small issues may signal big trouble ahead.* So it's very important that you don't stick your head in the sand, but actually pay attention to early warning signs.

Many large-scale business failures (whether companywide or in one small business unit) have long incubation periods, meaning that leaders have ample time to intervene when small problems arise, thereby avoiding a catastrophic outcome. Yet these small problems often go unnoticed, or someone sees them but doesn't want to "deal with it". That is why it is so important for you to not lead by fear! If your employees are scared to tell you things because you always yell or threaten them, they won't. You'll create an environment where you don't know much about what's really happening, and you'll spend your career-playing defense versus offense. And, trust me; being *proactive* tends to be a lot easier than being *reactive.*

View Problems as Opportunities

Most individuals and organizations do not view problems in a positive light. They perceive problems as abnormal conditions or situations that one must avoid at all costs. After all, fewer problems mean a greater likelihood of achieving the organization's goals and objectives. As a result, many leaders do not enjoy discussing problems, and they certainly do not cherish the opportunity to disclose problems in their own department. They worry that others will view them as incompetent for allowing the problem to occur, or incapable of resolving the problem on their own.

Smart leaders, and/or organizations, perceive problems quite differently. They view small failures as quite ordinary and normal. They recognize that problems happen, even in very successful organizations, despite the best leadership talent and most sophisticated management techniques. These organizations actually **embrace problems to promote innovation.**

Good leaders view problems as opportunities to **learn and improve**. Thus, they **seek out problems**, rather than sweeping them under the rug. Don't be a sweeper!

13 Leadership Tips for Problem Solving:

1. Leaders First Envision Success: Leaders know that every problem has an answer; it just needs to be found. Worrying about the problem gets you nowhere, while working towards the answer will get you everywhere. Leaders control their attitude and focus on results.

2. Leaders Clarify the Problem: Leaders determine what's wrong by cutting through clutter and noise, and by focusing on the issues that are at the core of the problem.

3. Leaders Get the Facts: Leaders collect all the facts about the problem because they know that some problems are not as big as they seem. Fact-finding is an analytical, rather than an emotional task, so it is useful in other ways, too. When a follower comes to a leader with a problem, a good leader will start asking questions and gather the facts, *rather than engage in an emotional discussion.* Fact-finding is a process and you may have to dig deep to get to the real problem. Leaders are great at asking the right fact-finding questions. They're also adept at listening to the answers and "hearing" any sub-text that could illuminate the situation.

4. Leaders Decide Which Problems Need Solving: Leaders don't guess or assume when it comes to problem solving. They decide where to focus their efforts based on the fact-finding step above. While every problem may have a solution, not every problem must be solved immediately. Leaders ask themselves: How bad is it? What is the worst that could happen if it this problem is ignored? Does it need to be fixed right away? It seems small, BUT what other things does this impact that could create a bigger issue? These questions help **put things in perspective**, and may reveal that the problem is not as worrisome as originally thought...or the opposite!

5. Leaders Start By Looking to Themselves for Possible Solutions: If the problem *does* need attention quickly, leaders first look to themselves for answers. They ponder what actions they might take personally that could resolve the problem. They brainstorm all ideas and write them down. If someone else developed the problem, they ask that person how *they think* it should be resolved. And if the issue is significant, the leader will go to their team, or trusted advisors, for idea sharing. Being able to get a variety of solutions to choose from, from people with different perspectives and experience, is powerful.

6. Leaders Continually Self-Evaluate: Leaders constantly assess whether the process is going well, if the solutions being discussed make sense, and if they are doing everything they can to solve the issue.

7. Leaders Do Research: Leaders consider what research would be valuable to their problem-solving efforts (like searching the Internet, asking other people, reading books, etc.). Leaders do not think of themselves as all knowing and understand that the first instinct for an answer is not necessarily the best. Sometimes when you are too knowledgeable about a subject, you can overlook something obvious.

8. Leaders Make Decisions: Leaders pick a solution and implement it. They may start with a quick-fix solution and follow up with a more long-lasting fix, but they decide what needs to be done...and they do it.

9. Leaders Follow Through: Effective leaders don't just implement the solution and turn away. They follow through with making sure necessary team members are also doing their part (if required). And they ask everyone involved how they think the "solution" is working out now that it's actually being used.

10. A Leader Can 'Let Go': A good leader can let go, but doesn't forget. Harboring the fear, embarrassment, anger, or frustration (whatever negative emotion the issue evoked) is counter-productive, so must be let go. But remembering how it came about, was resolved, and how *you* handled the situation (for future reference), is key.

11. Leaders Create Achievable Markers: Leaders break the problem-solving process into small objective steps, and then focus on the most immediate steps. They know how to break problems down into their component tasks and then track the progress of each one over measure.

12. Leaders Track Results: Test and monitor any solutions you implement. Don't just assume you're done. Despite your best intentions, any solution you implement might not work and can even make things worse!

13. Leaders Aren't Too Proud to Say "I'm Wrong": Be ready to undo whatever (ineffective) solution you implemented without shame. A respected leader is never embarrassed to correct mistakes. Without mistakes no progress would ever be made!

Lisa's Closing Comments:

Great leaders do not simply know how to solve problems; *they know how to find them.* They can detect smoke, rather than always fight raging fires. That's the type of leader I encourage you to be. Have a good rapport with your team, don't make them fearful of you, and encourage them to share bad news, red flags, or concerns with you *quickly!*

And, please note this: I've come across many *ineffective* leaders who try to pass-the-buck by placing the blame on their peers or employees. They act like small children on a playground when confronted by an adult after a toy is broken; all of them point fingers at each other. But when you're a boss and something in your department or team is "broken", and *your supervisor* asks you how or why it happened, <u>you must own it</u>.

You can point fingers at anyone you want, and make up every excuse in the book, but ultimately it's your fault because it happened on your watch. You will do nothing but look foolish in the eyes of your superiors if you sit there placing the blame on everyone else.

Don't be *that* type of leader. You'll lose the respect of your entire team and the respect of your boss. Take ownership of the issue, respect your team, look for solutions, and solve the problem. And in the process you'll continue to build, strengthen and solidify your Personal Leadership Brand!

CHAPTER SIX
The Ethical Essentials of Leadership

Thanks to the broken moral compass of high profile leaders in places like Wall Street, corporations, and government, the positive public perception of leadership is at an all-time low. So your goal should be to turn that around in how you conduct yourself.

Your personal ethics and values are another piece of your Personal Leadership Brand puzzle. Do people perceive you as "ethical" or "not-so-ethical"? Or maybe you are perceived as ethical but you really aren't. If so, creating a positive "real" Personal Leadership Brand will eventually be impossible because it has to be based on being your authentic self, all the time — even when no one is watching. And if behind-the-scenes you're different than what people see it will eventually come out.

Look how that scenario impacted high profile Ponzi-scheme criminal, Bernie Madoff. He's a great example of how trying to have two different Personal Brands, one good and one bad, rarely works out...for long.

So if you struggle with your own ethics, and feel you live a Jekyll and Hyde life like Bernie did, I strongly recommend going to therapy to figure out why and make some changes in your life. I have many real-world stories about typical employees, in companies probably like yours, that ended up losing everything because the possessed a damaged moral compass.

Ethical Questions

At its most basic, **ethics** is about deciding what is right (or *more* right) in a particular situation...determining what ought to be...and deciding what is consistent with one's personal or organizational value system. **Ethical leadership** combines ethical decision-making and ethical behavior, and occurs in both an individual and an organizational context.

The discipline of ethics begins with Socrates' question: *How should one live?* Ethics is about choice. What values guide us? What standards do we use? What principles are at stake? And how do we choose between them? An ethical approach to a problem will inquire about *goals and means* (the instruments we use to achieve these goals) and the *relationship between the two.*

The Values of Ethics

Values exist at the core of human nature. They are the building blocks of our belief system. Ethics are actions that reveal our values within an operating environment. If we say we cherish (value) a clean environment, but continue to pollute (abuse) it, our values and our ethical behavior *are incongruent.* Within a leadership role, the same is true of our attitude toward workers. Recent history of organizational failure underscores how placing **personal greed over expressed organizational values** destroys businesses and worse, destroys the faith workers have in business leaders. Hello, Enron. Hello, WorldCom. Hello, Madoff.

So, today, a major responsibility of a successful business leader must be to make ethical decisions and behave in ethical ways… and hopefully the overall organization **understands and practices its ethical code, too.**

Sound easy? Unfortunately "temptation" is always around the corner, and has caused some people with a strong moral code to sway and go to the dark side. We see those leaders everyday on the news (priests, politicians, CEO's, cops, football coaches, etc.) and there are many more we never see but who are getting caught, being fired, and/or going to jail, based on their misconduct.

Greed, fear and *desperation* are individually very powerful emotions that make people do stupid things…but when they are combined, the outcomes can be catastrophic. Example: Wall Street guy gets greedy because he sees what his friends have. He starts doing unethical things to make more money faster. Then he buys three houses, four cars, etc. And then, when s/he starts to see things get tough (like a market shift), s/he gets scared (*fear*), and *desperate* because s/he doesn't want to lose everything, and s/he starts to do things that are even more unethical.

And once you start going down some of these paths, there is no turning back. You're in, regardless of how much guilt you feel or regret you have. Once a line has been crossed, it's either turn yourself in (not necessarily to the cops, but perhaps admitting something to your boss), or keep the façade going.

Ethics Is As Ethics Does

Ethics are the *outward display of values.* When you have clarified *your own personal value system* and have a sense of your organization's values, then ethical behavior for you will be the **actions that are consistent with these values.** Leaders who "walk their talk" and act in accordance with the values they profess, are seen as people of integrity and of strong moral character.

Character is judged, at least partially, on the basis of integrity...and a person's integrity is made *tangible* by their actions! This is why being very clear on your "true" Personal Leadership Brand not only helps you manage what you say, but what you do, consistently.

Five Ethical Essentials All Leaders Must Embrace:

1. Choose actions that are consistent with 'the road you choose to travel' in your personal life: A clear personal purpose is the foundation for ethical professional behavior.

2. Behave in ways that make you proud: Self-esteem is a powerful tool for behaving ethically. Self-esteem is personal pride mixed with a fair amount of humility, and this balance creates the confidence to "hang tough" when dealing with *ethical dilemmas* (the temptations mentioned earlier).

3. Be patient and have faith in your decisions and yourself: Patience helps us to behave in ways that will be the best in the long run, thus avoiding the trap of bending your ethics for short-term gain.

4. Behave with persistence: This means behaving ethically all of the time — not just when it is *convenient to do so*. An ethical leader consistently sticks to his/her purpose to achieve what he/she envisions.

5. Behave in ways that are consistent with what is *really* important: This means keeping perspective. Perspective allows us to reflect and to see things more clearly so that we can see what is really important to guide our behavior.

There's a moral theory called **utilitarianism,** which says *the right action is the action that maximizes overall usefulness (utility)*. Utility is how leaders justify bending their ethics and breaking the rules. However, to maintain credibility and inspire follower-ship, leaders cannot make ethical exceptions of themselves. Being consistent is another piece in building your Personal Leadership Brand puzzle!

A Question of Trust

Trust is a key and basic component to any relationship. Unfortunately, trust is in very short supply these days. Many executives and senior leaders are unclear themselves as to their own roles and to their own futures. In the meantime, beneath them (the actual workforce itself), is functioning in a similar atmosphere of fear and powerlessness. They're suspicious of the people above them, creating a "you vs. us" mentality that kills an organization's ability to effectively function.

The study of ethics is a study of right vs. wrong, and how those types of decisions impact human relationships. Ethics define what we should do, and what we should be like as human beings, as members of a group or society, and in the different roles that we play in life...such as our roles in a business setting. Leadership is a particular type of ethical relationship marked by *power and/or influence, vision, obligation, and responsibility*.

By understanding the ethics of the leader-follower relationship, we gain a better understanding of leadership itself because some of the central issues in ethics are also the central issues of leadership. They include the personal challenges of authenticity, self-interest, and self-discipline, and moral obligations related to justice, duty, competence, and the greater good.

Ethics are Inspirational

An essential element of leadership is the ability to inspire others to follow by instilling in them optimistic *faith in the competency and ethical "compass" of the person in charge.* Sadly, decades of managerial malfeasance, corporate greed, and the recent economic meltdown has made workers anything but optimistic.

Mistrustful of the ethics and morals of those in charge, 21st Century employees have become jaded and angry towards leadership. According to a special report published by Bentley University's Center for Ethics, entitled *The 2011 National Business Ethics Survey*, 42% of the 4500+ employees surveyed said: Companies have weak ethics cultures. That's horrible and I believe it's your responsibility to play a part in reducing that percentage!

Be Seen and Heard

Even in good times, most senior leaders...especially in large organizations...are hardly visible to the rank and file. Tucked away in the executive suites, many leaders are unknown commodities to the people who are expected to follow them. With the exception of an annual corporate function or a disembodied video 'town hall' rah-rah session, top-level leaders are rarely seen or heard.

Good leaders need to be seen and they need to let their values be heard. During World War II, one of the most effective military leaders was Field Marshall Rommel. One of his key leadership attributes was that he frequently visited, talked and ate with the front line troops. His actions were humanizing, thus making him "one of us" to the troops serving beneath him.

So don't hide in your office or cubicle. Do not be afraid to talk with your staff honestly, alerting them to anticipated changes, and preparing them for continuous, unforeseen challenges. Be visible, approachable, and personable, and avoid creating a team where it is "you vs. them".

Six Practical Reasons an Ethical Workplace Matters

Many people are used to reading about or hearing of the **moral benefits** of fostering good business ethics. However, there are other types of benefits, as well, that are tangible, practical, and focused on an organization's success. These include:

1. Attention to business ethics has substantially improved society: Ethical business decisions have led to the abolition of child labor, unfair hiring practices, price fixing, etc. And they have led to the development of oversight groups, regulatory agencies, and increased community involvement by local businesses.

2. Ethics help maintain a moral course in turbulent times: During times of change, there is often no clear moral compass to guide leaders through complex conflicts about what is right or wrong. Continuing attention to ethics in the workplace sensitizes leaders and staff to how they want to act – with humanity and for the greater good.

3. Ethics cultivate strong teamwork and productivity: Ongoing attention and dialogue regarding values in the workplace builds openness, integrity and community, and those are critical ingredients to having a strong team in the workplace. When employees feel strong alignment between their values and those of their leader and organization, they react with strong loyalty and performance.

4. Ethics support employee growth: Attention to ethics in the workplace helps employees face reality, both good and bad, in the organization and themselves. These provide an opportunity for workers to self-correct and re-align with company values if they (the employee) are starting to behave unethically.

5. Ethics are an insurance policy: Attention to ethics ensures highly ethical policies and procedures in the workplace. It's far better to incur the cost of mechanisms to ensure ethical practices now than to incur costs of litigation later.

6. Ethics promote a strong public image: Attention to ethics is also strong public relations, although certainly ethical behavior should not be done primarily for reasons of public relations. Still, an organization that regularly gives attention to its ethics can portray a strong positive to the public. People see those organizations as valuing people more than profit, as striving to operate with the utmost of integrity and honor. And that positive image is manifested by the company's leadership and employees; at all levels!

Lisa's Closing Comments:

I think this is one of the most important chapters in the book. Why? Because! Many of the other chapter topics are things that you can learn, or become better at, with practice. But your ethics and personal integrity have to come from your *personal being.*

If your communication skills aren't great, you can work on those. And your boss may mention it to you, but you won't necessarily get in trouble over it (unless you choose not to work on those skills). However, if you do something unethical, even just once, you could not only lose your job, but possibly go to prison. Steal from the company? You could go to jail and ruin your career. Lie to customers for financial gain? You could get fired, and depending on the level of what you've done, possibly go to jail. Sabotage a co-worker for personal gain? This could lead to being fired;ruining your reputation (brand) at work, or even getting sued.

Basically, anything you choose to do that does not follow a strong code of personal ethics could become a very big, life altering, negative experience for you. But, it starts with the small stuff:

Calling in sick when you're really not; telling little white lies to cover yourself on a project being late; making promises to your team and not keeping them (like constantly cancelling one-on-ones with your staff members...employees complain to me about that a lot).

CHAPTER SEVEN
Employee Engagement & Retention

It is a common belief that competitors present the biggest threat to business success. The fact is that a threat that exists *within* a company itself trumps any outside forces. And what is one of the biggest threats your company or department may face that you may have to deal with as a leader? Unhappy employees!

Workers who have become disenchanted with their jobs can create havoc in a company with internal sabotage, large and small. They can also quit and take company secrets with them...possibly to your competition or to become competitors themselves. The best way to combat this internal threat is with strategies to keep the best and brightest among your employees satisfied.

Thus, focusing on employee rewards and recognition may be the wisest business decisions any company and leader can make. Do you know the top reason a person leaves a job is due to lack of rewards and recognition? Sure, pay, benefits, job satisfaction, etc. are all in the Top Ten reasons, but on average, lack of rewards and recognition rank the highest. When a person doesn't feel appreciated and valued, they eventually leave to go somewhere they do.

Ask bosses what makes employees happy at work, and many are likely to think in terms of tangible rewards: a good salary, time off, a pleasant office, generous benefits. However, ask employees themselves, and increasingly the "happiness factor" depends heavily on intangibles, such as *respect, trust, and fairness.*

But when focusing on rewards such as bonuses, recognition ceremonies, etc., it is wise to remember that a fundamental truth about employee retention is that employees who are satisfied with their work *and with their immediate supervisor* are more likely to classify themselves as "happy" and less likely to jump ship...*regardless of compensation.*

And it's important to note that particular forms of compensation "rewards" come and go with the times. Stock options had great cachet in the 1990s until the bubble burst. And filling retirement funds with company stock seemed great until Enron and others went bust. So it's important to understand that the *value* of rewards must be judged by a different standard. This has special significance in today's multi-generational workforce. As a leader, it's imperative to understand, that to be effective, a reward must be tailored to be meaningful to the recipient. But what does that mean?

It means that a one-size-fits-all rewards system isn't effective. What you might perceive as a great reward, someone else may not. That is why it's so important that you truly get to know each of your employees as individuals, and learn what excites and motivates each one of them.

Your company may already have a set rewards program in place, but that doesn't mean you can't create your own ideas for your team, too. And if your company does not have a rewards program in place, then you really need to create one for your group.

Being known as a boss or a co-worker who cares about and appreciates others, is yet ANOTHER key personality attribute your Personal Leadership Brand should include!

Reward Your Team!

The subject of employee rewards has been studied in great detail and a library of literature exists on the subject. One great example is the latest book by employee expert, Bob Nelson, entitled: *1501 Ways to Reward Employees* (Workman Publishing Company, March/2012). I strongly recommend that you pick up a copy! In it, he mentions the advantages of *creating employees who are so filled with an internal fire for success that managers and supervisors don't have to constantly light a fire under them.*

Yet, somehow, it doesn't come so easily for most managers, leaders, and organizations. Many can't figure out the right ingredients for job satisfaction, thus leading to higher turnover and unrealized productivity potential. For other companies, creating a rewards program (or just fostering a rewards *culture*) seems expensive and difficult to directly connect to bottom-line results.

For years, employers focused on handing out perks such as pay raises, performance bonuses, extra vacation time, and even preferential treatment (i.e. the coveted corner office or weekend at the company condo). These motivators aren't necessarily bad ideas, but are rather *short-term solutions* that inevitably lead to an eventual drop in performance again. After all, how motivating is a bonus check or vacation that's eight months away? For many people, not very!

Again, this is all about making your employees and co-workers feel valued and respected, often. So to only express your happiness and appreciation for them once a year (with a trip or bonus check), or during their "required" quarterly or bi-annual review,isn't often enough!

Two decades of research tells us that dangling carrots like this can't create a sustained shift in employee engagement and productivity. So what can? *Consistently* rewarding employees and co-workers, and sincerely expressing your gratitude and appreciation!

Understanding *what* rewards motivate your team members is essential to being a successful young leader, but you must also know *how* to give it to them; and that takes both will and skill. Quite honestly, most managers are uncomfortable handing out praise, or even just saying "Thank you" to their team members.

Luckily, the reality is that employee rewards are cost-effective and easy to implement on a daily basis. Plus, low-cost and no-cost rewards deliver a tremendous ROI (return on investment) with regard to employee satisfaction, and that translates into productivity and retention!

Let's now jump into ten ideas you can easily implement. And, as I mentioned before, pick up a book or two that offer tons of ideas. You're sure to find a few strategies that work really well for you!

Ten Ideas to Increase Retention by Rewarding (Groups & Individuals):

So, what rewards do matter to employees? Well, the best place to start is to ask your employees directly how they would like to be recognized and rewarded. The insights they provide may open your eyes to a variety of opportunities available and enable you to more effectively demonstrate that you appreciate their contributions to the workplace.

But to get your creativity bubbling, here are some popular ideas other companies and managers use to recognize and reward their employees:

Reward #1: Letters of Acknowledgement: A formal, informal, or semi-formal employee recognition letter works wonders. A message that points to specific contributions the employee made (related to a project or situation) goes a long way in helping employees feel recognized and rewarded, AND helps reinforce the desired behavior. In fact, a semi-formal employee recognition letter that includes a bonus check or a gift card (for a place or product you *know they like*; not something you "think" they like) magnifies the recognition an employee experiences.

Reward #2: Autonomy: Give employees the freedom to move around within their position, without sacrificing job performance. Employees who feel some ownership over their positions care more about what they do and feel more responsible for its success.

- Give employees the freedom to work independently (not micromanaged)

- Give employees flexibility in work hours (where position allows)

- Allow individuals to develop/improve processes for accomplishing tasks (where appropriate)

Reward #3: Professional Development/Advancement: Having knowledgeable and competent employees is a key to success. Providing them with the tools and opportunities to increase and hone their skills gives you a more qualified staff to work with.

• Allow staff to take advantage of formal training opportunities

• Allow staff to utilize the new skills they learn as soon as possible

• Give employees the opportunity to brief others on what they learned in training

• Provide in-house training and cross-training opportunities

Important Factoid: According to the 2011 Pricewaterhouse-Cooper's Global CEO Survey: *"For Millennials (aka: Gen Y), training and development is the most highly valued employee benefit. The number choosing training and development as their first choice of benefit is THREE times higher than those who chose cash bonuses. And 98% surveyed believe working with strong coaches and mentors is an important part of their development"*. This is important to know if you're responsible for managing and retaining Millennial talent. They are telling you what they want!

Reward #4: Fun: Doing something fun once in a while allows employees to let go of the stresses of the day (or week or month) and re-energize themselves to be more productive! This can also create better relationships within the office if employees are allowed to "goof around" with their workmates. Other *fun* things include:

• Write positive comments on Post-It notes and leave them for employees to find

• Give team members Silly String to let off a little steam during high stress times

• Provide opportunities to laugh and socialize

• Throw lunch parties to celebrate special events

Reward #5: Provide Meaningful Work: There are tasks to everyone's job that are less enjoyable than others, but there may be opportunities to assign work that is challenging, fun and/or meaningful to the employee which furthers the department in reaching their goals. Of course, the less enjoyable tasks must still be done, but providing opportunities for a variety of tasks may enhance the job enough to make those "other" duties less tedious.

• Recognize individual talents and interests when assigning work projects

• Let staff cross train on other functions

• Allow for some variety of job duties which may break up the monotony

• Rotate interesting projects among employees

• Ask employees what else they'd like to be doing/trying to be more satisfied at work

Reward #6: Empowerment: Employees don't necessarily want to *run* the department, but they may like to contribute to "bettering" the department. This makes them feel a part of something and that their opinions matter. You, as their manager, or other supervisors, will make the final decision, but employee insights may help broaden your perspective.

• Ask staff directly for their opinions and ideas (individually and in meetings)

• Encourage them to provide you feedback at any time

- Have staff participate on committees and in meetings

- Recommend your employees to others as a resource or subject matter expert

- Assign staff projects which draw on employees' ideas and creativity

Reward #7: Prizes: Little prizes can go a long way in saying "thanks" even if the monetary value is not high. Be creative and customize the prizes that you are giving to the employee that you are giving it to. This lets your employees know that you recognize and appreciate their work and that you are interested in them as individuals. Prizes can be given for completing special projects, making significant departmental improvements and contributions, reaching goals, and other noteworthy accomplishments.

- Gift certificates (cannot be redeemable for cash)

- Candy Bars

- Concert tickets to see someone you know they love

Reward #8: Recognition: Employees should know how much their work is being valued – by their supervisor and by their department. While recognition need not be done by means of a lavish ceremony, it should be done quickly and clearly. Employees should know what they are being recognized for and be encouraged to continue contributing in a positive way.

- Hold special meetings regularly to celebrate successes and special events (Service Awards, special accomplishment awards, etc.)

- Create a "Thank You" board where *employees* can post thank you notes *for other employees* (i.e.: Mike! Thanks for staying late last night with me to get the project done!)

• Name a space in a department after an employee and put up a sign

• Develop your own departmental award program and create a certificate/trophy. *Example: One manager bought a $2 plate, painted it gold, wrote a silly award name on it, and employees vie to get that plate all the time. To have it on your desk has become a "big deal" in their department.*

Reward #9: Time Off: Many people would appreciate an unexpected "Great job! Take Monday off!" type of reward (versus a small bonus check or gift card). We all like time off! And it's easy to implement and much appreciated!

Reward #10: Commemorative Gifts: These are *small tokens* that you can give to your employees that will recognize the things that they have done for you. This is different than giving them a monetary bonus, because it is actually giving them something that they can *display and be proud of.* Things along these lines are: *Good quality* engraved plaques, pens, watches, desk clocks, etc. And I'm not referring to tacky promotional items with your company logo all over it! I'm referring to items of good quality that you can personalize for each person.

Lisa's Closing Comments:

One of the most frequently asked questions submitted to the Society of Human Resource Management website is: *"How do we keep talent from jumping to our competitors?"*

Now, combine that question with a popular saying that I mentioned before: *"People don't leave their companies; they leave their managers (or people)".*

See? The pressure on managers to retain their talent is huge. Companies that can retain the best talent, the longest, at any position level, will do the best. Although many companies offer terrific *company-wide* policies, perks, and reward programs, the power of those things wear off quickly if someone is stuck with a manager they don't like, and with one who never expresses gratitude. Things like benefits, company cars, stock options, expense accounts, travel, interesting work, company parties, room for advancement, etc. ALL become meaningless (after a period of time) if the person's day-to-day manager is a chump. And being unappreciative, or being *unable to express gratitude and kudos,* are typically leading "chump" qualities.

Here's the deal: It used to be that strong leadership meant the ability to motivate employees. But the reality is that most employees are motivated and want to do a great job; it is **work environments that de-motivate** them. When managers consistently fail to provide the direction, resources, respect and recognition that employees require, their **innate desire to achieve** diminishes and becomes re-directed (typically to another job).

Throughout this book so far I've shared tips and strategies that can help you manage, lead, and work with people more effectively. Communication strategies, attributes of effective leaders, and problem solving strategies are all examples. And all of that info was geared to help you assess your strengths and weaknesses so that you can improve, or create, a stronger Personal Leadership Brand.

But those insights don't matter much if you can't retain your employees, or if you have constant dissention with your co-workers! Like I mentioned earlier, the leading reason people leave their jobs is due to lack of (regular/frequent) recognition. And the responsibility of that falls on you if you manage employees.

So make your employees and/or co-workers feel appreciated and respected on a regular basis, and the respect for *your* Personal Leadership Brand will skyrocket!

CHAPTER EIGHT
Successful Senior Executives Share 40 Quick Tips

A lot of the business events I attend I'm participating in some way: either as a speaker, panelist, moderator, facilitator, etc. But sometimes I get the pleasure of just "attending" as an audience member and I get to watch everyone else do the work.

FountainBlue presented one such gathering and it was their monthly "When She Speaks, Women in Leadership Series" event. There were two things that motivated me to go on that Friday afternoon: The topic for one, plus my friend and colleague, Camille Smith, was moderating the panel.

The panel discussion was entitled: *Leading With Power, Influence and Integrity*, and a lot of the panel discussion quickly began to focus on the importance of Personal Branding.

Their panel was comprised of female executives from different large corporations (names of panelists and their companies needed to be withheld in this book due to their employers' legal policies):

Facilitator: Camille Smith, Founder/President, Work In
    Progress Coaching, Inc.
Panelist: VP of Global Services
Panelist: Principal Scientist (senior executive position)
Panelist: Senior Vice President of HR
Panelist: Senior Director Program Management & FPLC

Here are 40 of their personal leadership tips and insights they shared that day pertaining to *Leading with Power, Influence and Integrity*. As you read their comments, you'll see how many of them map directly to "attributes and reputation", and that IS Personal Branding:

1. Power, influence and integrity *are three inter-connected circles* that create the foundation for being an effective leader.

2. Whereas there are many ways to describe *power*, the concept of *integrity* is more nebulous. It refers to a concept of wholeness, of alignment with your personal values, as well as that of your organization and your team.

3. Defining leadership moments are not easy. There will be conflict, resistance, and difficult circumstances. You may test a relationship, or even jeopardize your job. If you are up to the task and doing the right thing based on your personal assessment and your personal moral standards, it will prepare you for more of these opportunities to learn and grow and lead.

4. Leading with power, influence and integrity takes the strength and intelligence to make plans and the courage to execute them, especially under difficult circumstances when many variables can impact the right course of action.

5. Leadership goes well beyond positional power, where someone has the authority to manage other people or projects and might rightfully use coercion as a strategy. People can also gain power by becoming an expert/authority on a specific topic by encouraging/reinforcing others around them.

6. If you have positional power, use that power judiciously.

7. Don't be someone you're not. Find your personal "voice" and define your personal brand/style at work.

8. Power is sharing info with people, not withholding it.

9. For every ONE point of "suggestion/constructive criticism" you offer to an employee, provide NINE compliments.

10. Empowerment and engagement are much more effective at getting things done and building positive relationships.

11. "Power over" is about coercion and being domineering. "Power to" is about affecting change. "Power with" is centered on collaboration. "Power Within" is centered on yourself.

12. Be willing to walk away from a company or client without integrity.

13. Never ask anyone to do something you wouldn't personally do.

14. Don't shrink from any conversations with yourself. *You must avoid denial with regards to any situation.* This can lead to small issues becoming huge ones – and people will then be asking you, "How and why did this happen?"

15. Embrace conflict *tactfully*: Speak-up (not in volume, but with your thoughts), debate with inquiry, and keep inquiring until there is nothing left to say.

16. Communicate with courage and confidence, *not intimidation.*

17. Insist on a seat at the table. Don't avoid *getting involved.*

18. People are listening to what you say…and to what you DON'T say.

19. Be *empathetic* to employee needs and desires.

20. Have your "core values" written down and share them with your team.

21. Be an expert. When faced with something you're not very familiar with, don't fake it. Take the time to research the topic/issue and get to really understand it. Only then can you be useful in the decision-making process.

22. Proactively manage your relationships with others, AND your relationship with yourself.

23. Power is having information – accurate information about anything. Don't go by rumors. Go to reliable sources and get solid information.

24. Focus on people. They are the most important assets you have.

25. Surround yourself with people who can support you and believe in you…and who are honest with you.

26. Interact with a lot of people at work regularly, and empower people to make decisions versus using your "power card" all the time. The key is to create an "inclusive environment" *versus a dictatorship.*

27. Empower your people, don't "de" power them. This will actually make your life easier.

28. Leadership is not painted in black and white. Be aware of the nuances of behaviors and interactions and manage accordingly.

29. Be passionate and hold to your true values, your personal moral standards.

30. It may be perceived that adhering to your moral standards would make you *less powerful,* but actually the opposite is true. When you act with integrity people take notice and give you more power, and that means you have more influence.

31. Figuring out what's right and wrong might not be as difficult as deciding between two good things.

32. Focus both on your core values and also on the core values of your organization. Ensure alignment when you're considering joining a company, and as you work for a company.

33. Consider strategically who will be impacted by actions and decisions made, and plan accordingly.

34. Bring a skill of value to the table.

35. Accept, but manage, your emotions. Most people are less effective at getting things done if too much emotion is distracting them from doing the tasks at hand or doing the strategic thinking needed to achieve objectives.

36. Say what you will do, and do what you say you will do.

37. Be the boss you want to have. *Would you want to work for you?*

38. *Leadership is about doing the right thing, even when no one's going to know.* – Oprah (a panelist quoted this)

39. *Have the discipline and control to influence your power over others' lives.* – Clint Eastwood (a panelist quoted this)

40. *Know when to hold 'em, know when to fold 'em.* – Kenny Rogers (a panelist quoted this)

Lisa's Closing Comments:

Well, there you go! 40 tips from highly successful, highly respected, senior executives. A different global corporation employed each panelist and each of them had 15+ years of workforce experience.

I hope you noticed a few common threads through much of what they shared, such as: respect your employees, lead with integrity and a moral compass, take responsibility for your actions, and learn from everyone and every situation.

Following these tips have worked well for them, so they can work well for you, too. And I strongly recommend reviewing their comments as you think about YOUR Personal Leadership Brand. Who ARE you now? And who do you ASPIRE to become?

Oftentimes, they are different, hence the reason for self-evaluation, being honest with yourself, and doing the necessary work to become who you WANT to be. You can't develop an *effective* Personal Leadership Brand until you know where you are and where you want to go!

Understanding Your Multigenerational Work Colleagues

"63% of top executives say that most Managers' careers are stalled because they simply <u>do not</u> understand others."

Across the Board Magazine (for Business Leaders)

INTRODUCTION TO PART TWO
Understanding Your Multigenerational Work Colleagues

My first two books focused on generational dynamics in the workforce. The first one was *Millennials Incorporated* and that was written to help companies and managers better recruit, manage and retain Millennial (aka: Gen Y) employees. My second book, *Millennials into Leadership*, was written FOR the Millennials on how to be young, respected leaders in the workforce. So, I've been pretty deep into learning about and understanding generations at work for quite some time.

As an expert in this area, well-known corporations hire me (a lot) to conduct seminars and workshops on improving generational dynamics at work, and preparing Millennials for leadership positions, because it's an issue for them. In a nutshell, generational dynamics in the workforce has truly become the "new" diversity challenge for many companies.

And if you think I'm making that up, think again. There's a reason that companies like Johnson & Johnson, eBay, Wells Fargo, and Paul Mitchell Systems have hired me, and continue to hire me, as a speaker and Thought Leader on this topic: It's real! One of my most popular seminars is "Improving Communication Across the Generations". It's always a lively session and one that all attendees, of any age, learn a lot from.

The reason I'm telling you all this is because, as we've discussed in previous chapters, effectively communicating with, and understanding, your co-workers is key for creating a respected Personal Leadership Brand. And one critical component to "understanding" your employees and co-workers better is to understand them from a *generational* perspective.

It's important for you to know what Boomers, Generation Jones, Gen X and Millennials (aka: Gen Y) are about. Generational differences can (and do) affect communication, problem solving, relationship building, retention, loyalty, and team morale. And, if/when you manage a team and your team suffers from a high turnover rate or low productivity rate, your company's top brass are going to look at you as the problem.

So the purpose of this section is to give you a brief snapshot about the employees, co-workers, and supervisors you may currently work with, or will work with, so that you can better understand why they are the way they are. These insights will also give you great tools for better engaging with each member of your multigenerational workforce.

And when you better understand people, it's obvious to everyone around you, and that reflects well on your Personal Leadership Brand!

Please Note: *The following information is based on broad generational similarities. Obviously not everyone is the same or shares the exact personal history and traits I'll be describing. But I can tell you that a vast majority of people who attend my presentations all totally relate to the descriptions I share about their generation(s)...and the ones they work with!*

CHAPTER NINE
Millennials (aka: Gen Y):
The Largest Generation in Our History

Millennial Birth Years (approx.):1980 to 2002

Millennial History & Overview

Here are some insights to consider: The Millennials graduating from college are members of the generation of kids raised with "Baby On Board" signs stuck to their parents' minivan window; using car seats and bike helmets were required when they were children; and when they were reaching puberty every state implemented some sort of driver's license law requiring additional "practice hours," and/or created laws limiting the amount of teens in a car, and/or enforced driving curfews for teens.

My teen years were spent packing 10 friends in a car and party hopping on weekends until late at night. And when I was a young kid riding a bike, the only thing between my skull and the asphalt was my hair. *My point?* This generation has been raised with laws to protect them more than any other generation in our history. So, our society and government, not just their parents, have been telling them they are "special and valued" since Day One.

The Millennials are also the first generation of kids in our history encouraged to talk openly about their feelings at school and at home. The philosophy of, "Children should be seen and not heard", was eliminated when the Millennial kids started arriving. Our country turned into a "pro kid" society when they were born, and this generation was immediately put on a pedestal, coddled, nurtured, and treated with respect by their Baby Boomer or Generation Jones parents.

As a result, many experts believe the average 10-year-old today is probably as mature and outspoken as the average 16-year-old was in the 1960s. Their parents respect their opinions and even seek their children's advice in major purchasing decisions for the family.

But why has this new generation of young professionals turned into such a hot commodity in the workforce? Why are stories about them all over the media? One key factor is the looming reality of the *Boomer Brain Drain* that companies across the country are going to feel over the next 5-15 years (starting now as the oldest Boomers hit retirement age). Here's one simple statistic, out of many, from the Office of Employment Projections that will quickly put this into perspective: *The average large company in the U.S. will lose 30-40% of its workforce due to retirement over the next 5-15 years.* Ouch.

And we have as many GenXers on the planet as there is going to be (and they're a small generation), so the head count replacement of this massive Boomer exodus are the Millennials. Therefore,recruiting and retaining them has turned into a big, competitive business and will continue to be, especially as the economy recovers.

Lisa's Closing Comments:

Now that you have a general idea of why companies are clamoring to hire them, I thought it would be a good idea to share a few key management tips with you. And, yes, when it comes to some of the management tips, I see some eyes roll from older generations who attend my seminars and workshops. But once I tell them that companies and management teams at companies like IBM, Wells Fargo, Toyota and Marriott spend a lot of time, effort and money on understanding Millennials, they quickly realize that it may be a good idea to at least consider what I'm suggesting. Notice I said, "suggest". What you do is up to you.

Management & Retention Tips:

1. Change Your Attitude: If you tend to have a gruff nature with employees, you may want to consider changing that a bit. Millennials won't tolerate it like your older colleagues may have. They'll leave. They expect to be treated with respect and spoken to professionally.

2. Become a Praise Culture: This is a generation that still got a trophy even if their soccer team came in last place. They have been praised from Day One. They expect rewards and praise often. And, as previously mentioned in this book, research has proven that by implementing a better recognition program, retention of ALL generations increases.

3. Offer Plenty of Face Time: A survey of Millennial professionals, conducted by Robert Half International and Yahoo! Hot Jobs, found that over 60% of Millennials want to communicate with their managers *at least once a day*. Basically, this generation does not do well with just monthly or quarterly review sessions. They want feedback daily to discuss how things are going and how they are performing.

So are the rumors you've heard about them being high maintenance true? Yes. But, they are also be high performing. Our workplaces have really started to feel their impact now that the eldest Millennials are hitting 30 years old. And, because they are such a huge generation, Millennials will occupy 75% of the workforce by 2025. That's huge!

Plus, this generation is rapidly redefining work environments, success, leadership, communication, management, entrepreneurship, corporate culture, and professional relationships. *Have YOU noticed the Millennial impact yet at your company? If not, you will!*

CHAPTER TEN

Gen X: A Small & Complex Generation

Gen X Birth Years (approx.):1966 to 1979

Gen X History & Overview

Factoid: *Many of the conflicts that occur in the workforce today tend to happen between Millennials and Generation X.* Part of the reason for this is that Millennials are close in age to them, so this tends to create more of a *sibling* dynamic, versus a *parental* dynamic (like Millennials often have with Boomers). And, they are close enough in age so they are often *competing* at work (for promotions, projects, recognition, etc.). But there are other reasons this (sometimes) challenging dynamic occurs, so let's discuss Gen X for a minute. You're bound to learn some insights that will help you as the leader of a team that includes Gen X employees.

Gen Xers were raised in the heart of the 1970's – a time in our society where divorce rates skyrocketed. And mothers, even those still married, embarked on careers and (many) stopped being "stay at home moms". This is the era when the term "Latchkey Kids" was created, and the kids behind the latches were the Xers. For those of you not familiar with the term, it refers to coming home from school at a young age, and because no parent(s) were home from work yet, they were instructed to lock the doors while they were home without an adult.

The shift in history Gen X experienced as kids and teens created a generation of young people who sought *family ties* with friends, and were forced to be independent and in a survival mode at an early age. And also during that time, our country was in the wake of the controversial Vietnam War and a severe economic bust. This had many of their parents raising Gen X kids with messages of "Be careful out there!" and "Don't trust authority!" and "Look out for yourselves!"

The result? Gen X is often viewed as a cynical generation. Being on the cusp of Gen X and Gen Jones myself, I can tell you that I can relate. When I discuss this in seminars, most of the Gen Xers nod along in agreement. So I'm not just making this up.

Gen Xers sometimes don't have the easiest time with "team work", and often scoff at having to attend management and leadership training seminars. As a whole, *they like to be left alone to do what they do, and how they like to do it.* They often possess a cocked eyebrow at authority, which can make it really challenging for their bosses – especially if the boss is younger than they are (15% of Managers are now currently Millennials).

Here's one other thing you possibly didn't know: Gen X introduced the term *work-life balance* into the workforce. Tired of watching the Boomers work endless hours, and even more tired of feeling like they needed to keep pace with them, their generation began to demand that employers respect an employee's life outside of work more. This whole concept seems to be getting more attention with Millennials entering the workforce – but know it was Gen X who started the work-life balance movement for everyone!

Lisa's Closing Comments:

As a whole, Gen X isn't big on chitchat, and they're not overly into being warm and fuzzy with co-workers or bosses. They prefer a direct communication style/dynamic, and when annoyed, their non-verbal cues can be pretty obvious (meaning, they typically don't hold back on rolling their eyes, sitting back and folding their arms, or saying something with an obvious "tone" in their verbal delivery). This tends to be very difficult for Millennials to deal with. In the workshops I conduct specifically for Millennial employees, they constantly tell me how they clash with their 30-something co-workers or boss.

One final important point to be aware of if you manage a team with Millennials and Gen X employees: A popular term created pertaining to the Millennial Generation was "Helicopter Parents". That was developed because their parents are/were always "hovering" over them to help with everything. So, can you see a difference between the terms for Gen X, "Latchkey Kids" (parents absent and being alone), versus "Helicopter Parents" (parents always helping and guiding them) for the Millennial's parenting experience? *It's pretty significant and drastically different!*

Hopefully that sheds some light on why many Gen Xers tend to resent Millennials, and why they oftentimes have an intense dislike for them. I'm not exaggerating when I say that. I've literally had 100+ Gen Xers tell me they truly have a very hard time with the Millennials they work with and don't like them. That sentiment is shared with me in just about every seminar I conduct that has Gen Xers in attendance.

So as someone who manages, or works on a team with both of those generations involved, it's good that you're now privy to this (often) challenging dynamic!

CHAPTER ELEVEN

Generation Jones: Who Are They?

Generation Jones Birth Years (approx.): 1954 to 1965

Gen Jones History & Overview

The term Generation Jones was coined and defined by a colleague of mine, Mr. Jonathan Pontell, a leading social commentator. According to the research he (and others) have shared, this demographic is defined by people born from 1954-1965 and they currently comprise the largest adult population in the US (26% = 53 million people). Prior to his research they had always been lumped together with the Boomer generation. But their upbringing and history was significantly different from the (older) Boomers (born between 1942-1953).

While many Boomers were protesting Vietnam, attending Woodstock, and kicking off the sexual revolution, Gen Jones was attending elementary school, and hanging out at home watching *The Brady Bunch*, playing Pong, and cooking with Easy Bake Ovens.

As a member of Gen Jones myself, I can say I was relieved when I came across Jonathan's research. I had never fully identified with either Gen X or the Boomers. But, depending on what generational birth range you looked at, I was either considered a really old Gen Xer or a really young Boomer. His research identifying Generation Jones expressed things I could totally relate to. My first reaction was, "Finally! I have a generational identity that really does describe *me!*"

Many Gen Jonesers were still too young to make an impact as leaders back in the turbulent 70's and booming 80's so they were forced to wait for their turn in the spotlight. And, now, that time has come. Born in 1961, President Obama is a Joneser like many senior executives in the workforce now are. His leadership style, and the personality traits we all witness in media interviews, is very similar to the Gen Jonesers who are my peers. A vast majority of them (us) seem to be: Calm yet yearning, direct yet respectful, personable yet professional, extremely approachable yet slightly distant, and very outwardly confidant yet internally obsessed in self-evaluation. Yep, that pretty much sums *me* up!

Many younger Jonesers were raised with a Mom at home and a Father working. And their early childhoods were filled with a sense of innocence. During the time my older Boomer cousins were in their teens or 20's protesting war, "experimenting" with pot or whatever, and getting caught up in Beatlemania, I was a young kid into riding my bike, skateboarding, and *jones-ing* to play Pong.

Lisa's Closing Comments:

In general, Gen Jonesers share a quiet optimism, confidence and patience. You'll find that they possess strong characteristics of both Gen X and Boomers: One day they'll want to "do lunch" with you, but the next they'll only want short, succinct communication with you. Sometimes they'll be focused on wanting to work as a team and then switch to wanting to work solo on a project. And from a work ethic standpoint, members of Gen Jones often follow the path of the Boomers – *they tend to be workaholics.* Ummm…I can relate to that!

I realize the overview I provided of Generation Jones may actually make them seem schizophrenic! But don't let that scare you when having to work with them. They tend to be fair, personable, diplomatic, and willing to go the extra mile. And their "traditional" Boomer-type values also foster loyalty in them as employees.

If you're younger than they are, focus on respecting their long-time professional experience, seek their input, value their knowledge, and maintain an honest dialogue with them about how you prefer to work, yet be open to how they do, too.

Please Note: For more detailed information about Generation Jones, I encourage you to visit Jonathan Pontell's website: GenerationJones.com.

CHAPTER TWELVE
Boomers: The Seasoned Players at Work

Boomer Birth Years (approx.): 1942 to 1953

Boomer History & Overview

The mass Boomer retirement (aka: Boomer Brain Drain) is something that will impact the workforce for decades, and it has started. Here are some fast facts to put this in perspective: From an article written in 2011, Samuel N. Asare, MBA, CRPC, CMFC states: *"...beginning January 1, 2011, and for the next 19 years, an estimated 10,000 Baby Boomers will turn age 65 daily! That's 1 Boomer reaching retirement age every 8 seconds for the next 19 years straight!"*

The amount of knowledge and experience going with them as they retire is something companies are scrambling to harness. Therefore, companies are also focused on recruiting and retaining Millennials (and other generations younger than Boomers) to build their future workforce, but a lot of time is also being spent on how to retain Boomers longer. Why? Not only do the companies need the headcount, but they also need them to share their knowledge with as many younger employees as possible.

Sure, many younger workers know how to bring new technology into the workforce at lightning speed (while many *older* Boomers have no desire to text or fully understand social media). But much of what they can teach younger employees,such as: navigating the political waters of the workforce, making wise career decisions, building relationships, learning the ropes on how to do their job at hand (marketing, engineering, accounting, HR, etc.), are invaluable.

So if you are not currently seeking a Boomer at work to be (one of) your Mentors, you're doing you and your career a HUGE disservice!

The Boomers began to arrive during a time when things in the U.S. were going really well. We were at the tail end of WWll, the economy was booming, and most Boomers spent their adolescence in the innocent 1950's. The term "nuclear family" was created during their generation, and referred to having a traditional family upbringing (a Mom at home and a Dad working).

During their developmental years, Boomers saw their parents stay at one job for a very long time, witnessed those companies take good care of their parent(s) in retirement, and saw the work ethic of their Veteran Generation parents and/or grandparents. This was an era where you worked hard, didn't complain, tolerated a job or (bad) boss even if you didn't love them, and felt loyalty towards the company that employed you.

As the Boomers began to enter the workforce, they brought these traditional values with them. There are many people over 50 years old who have been at the same company for 25+ years. So this changing workforce dynamic of "moving around to new jobs a lot", and companies not being loyal to *their employees*, is extremely unsettling to many of them.

Lisa's Closing Comments:

Many Boomers "grew up" in the workforce at a time when you didn't question authority. You did your job and kept your mouth shut. Because of this, younger generations have a hard time adjusting to the common Boomer personality trait of "putting process ahead of results". This means that even though you may have a more efficient way of doing something, a Boomer may be more concerned with keeping the process as-is because "that's the way the company has done it for years".

But on a positive note, Boomers also tend to be much like Millennials in terms of being personable and optimistic. They also enjoy relationship building, and appreciate business invitations to have lunch or dinner. Remember, they were doing martini lunches when it wasn't frowned upon, so don't hesitate to offer invitations to them for socializing outside of the office.

And again, their values tend to make them very loyal and willing to go the extra mile at work. So, if you manage or work with people between 56-67 years old, they could be the most loyal and hard working team members you'll have.

If you're a Millennial don't disregard a Boomer's input just because you think they're "out of touch" on the latest tech gadgets or social media worlds. They bring much more to the table than technical expertise (or lack thereof). Again, you can learn, *and will learn*, from team members who have 25+ more years of work experience than you do.

As a leader with Boomer employees, I recommend that you consider setting up a *reverse mentor program*. I've suggested this to many clients and it works really well. This means you team-up younger employees with Boomers, and they can assist the Boomers with learning new technology solutions your company implements, understanding different social media strategies, reviewing new tech tools for communication and productivity, etc.

You can also arrange casual *lunch & learn* workshops where employees provide training on new technology, and invite *any* employees to attend (not just Boomers). There are many people younger than Boomers who also struggle with technology and learning new processes, so make a comfortable, non-judgmental, environment for *everyone* to learn in.

Factoid: It's a proven medical fact that most of us begin to lose our ability to *quickly and easily* learn new complex processes and tools past the age of 45. Plus, it becomes more of a challenge as we push 60. So for all you employees under 35 years old please be mindful of this and support your Boomer team members with some additional patience and understanding...and you'll quickly see how it positively impacts your Personal Leadership Brand!

How to Create a Unique Personal Leadership Brand

"Your Personal Brand tells people who you are, and what they can expect from you. Effective executives, both men and women, proactively build & manage their brands. Indeed, your Personal Brand can limit, or launch, your career success."

Chief Operations Officer @ Fortune 500 Company

"Having a defined Personal Brand can take you far – even farther than you had originally envisioned – and more likely so if you actively manage it."

Sr. Globalization Business Manager @ Fortune 1000 Company

INTRODUCTION TO PART THREE

Why do "conventional" employees, who are not aspiring to be mainstream celebrities, professional athletes, or politicians, go through the trouble of creating a strategic Personal Leadership Brand? Well, let's look at the four main career benefits of doing so:

Differentiation: A Personal Leadership Brand differentiates you from others – it enables you to stand out among your workforce "competition" and therefore be more memorable. A Personal Leadership Brand conveys your identity and distinctiveness as an employee and communicates the value you offer to your employees, peers, and supervisors.

Consistency: A Personal Leadership Brand ensures that you are consistent – that is, you are reliable and act the same in most situations, which creates trust with co-workers. People know what to expect from you because you communicate and act from the same platform regardless of circumstance, and that builds a reputation that people will come to rely on.

Clarity: When you have a Personal Leadership Brand, you stand for something. People around you are clear on your values, and YOU are clear on your values. As with any brand (personal, product or company), everything you do and every decision you make, will start with asking yourself: "If I do this (or act like this, respond like this, say it like this, etc.), will it be supporting, or diluting, and/or mapping to, my Personal Leadership Brand?" You can also see how asking questions like this can help keep your moral compass on the right path!

Authenticity: Lastly, having a defined Personal Leadership Brand allows you to speak with authenticity. Your Personal Leadership Brand communicates who you really are, not someone you really are not. When an employee's verbal and non-verbal communication truly maps to who they are they are much more persuasive than when they are emulating a fake persona. Here's what one extremely successful executive shared with me pertaining to that: *"Don't be someone you're not. Find your personal 'voice' and define your OWN personal brand/style at work."*

Trying to live life putting up a "front", either in your personal or professional life, is exhausting. And, by the way, most people know when you're doing it (or they eventually always find out). SO JUST BE YOU. You have special traits, values, and strengths to offer...and the workforce and world will welcome you/them!

Now, let's get into strategically developing *your* Personal Leadership Brand...

CHAPTER THIRTEEN

Personal Branding Demystified: What It Is…and Is Not!

The benefit of consciously shaping a Personal Leadership Brand is *focus*; when you know with utmost clarity what you want to be known for, and who you *really are*, it is easier to let go of the behaviors, actions, projects, employees, and even job offers, that do not map to your brand platform.

Let me start by explaining what a personal brand is NOT:

1. It's not your title
2. It's not your business card
3. It's not your job description
4. It's not how you look

These are all things that <u>support and reflect</u> your brand. *So… what IS a Personal Leadership Brand?* It is a person's emotional feeling *about you* and it is a promise for a specific experience *with you*. Your brand *touches everything* pertaining to you…everything you say and don't say and everything you do and don't do.

A key concept that I strongly recommend burning into your brain is this:

When someone has contact with your brand, one of two things happens: your brand is reinforced…or it is weakened.

This is why it is so important to know what your brand value, brand positioning, brand promise, and brand personality are. They need to be reinforced and reflected in everything you say, do, and create.

And, for those of you who have (or will have) employees or contractors working for you, they need to be aware of your brand promise and values, too. As the leader, you're the **brand evangelist**

of your group or company, and that means making sure anyone working for you focuses on also positively reinforcing your brand... not weakening it. Basically, they are not only representing themselves, but they are also representing you.

One of the best things you can do to create a positive brand platform is focus on being *people-centric*. Always be open to listening to feedback, have a top-to-bottom commitment to making your customers, employees and co-workers your #1 priority, and always look at your decisions from their perspective.

Think about it as a consumer of products...you're a customer for a wide variety of products and services. Why are YOU loyal to their brand(s)? I bet it's probably because they promise a specific experience with their product or service and *consistently deliver on it*. So if you can make a person's experience with your Personal Leadership Brand *consistently* consistent with your brand promise, you are heading down the right path.

But how do you get the ball rolling on understanding you and what you want to be known for? Keep reading!

CHAPTER FOURTEEN

3 Steps to Create Your Unique Personal Brand Platform (with exercises)

I hope after reading the previous chapter you have a better understanding of the concept of branding. Certainly I realize it's not a super simple one; otherwise clients wouldn't hire me to help them with theirs and I wouldn't be asked to conduct so many workshops about this for employee groups!

But if you can really focus on what I've shared thus far and make the effort to follow the info I'll be sharing in this chapter, you CAN create a unique Personal Leadership Brand platform for yourself. And once you've come up with what you think works, I recommend running your concept by trusted clients, friends, and/or colleagues for their honest feedback.

Also consider doing this process as a group activity with your team members. The more clarity everyone has about themselves, and each other, the better!

I've had quite a few managers do that and it's an effective, fun activity that can really open up some interesting, useful dialogue amongst your team and foster team building. There's NO downside to everyone getting more clarity about themselves and their co-workers.

Okay, let's get started on the 3 Steps to Creating a Unique Brand Platform...

STEP ONE: Define Your Core Uniqueness & Determine Your Value Add

STEP ONE OVERVIEW: This step is to give you the big picture on *who* you are and *what* your *value* is. The exercise below is courtesy of my good friend and colleague, Sherry Prescott-Willis, who is also a marketing expert and author. I modified it to be for employees versus small businesses (as she had originally created it), and it's from her popular book on Amazon, *MarketThis! An Effective 90-Day Marketing Tool* (www.MarketThisBook.com).

EXERCISE 1: YOUR CORE UNIQUENESS & VALUE ADD

Example: Adrian Jessup, Marketing Manager (Fictional Employee)

The core purpose of my expertise and role at work is...

Helping my employer: Build its brand recognition, launch new products/services, manage products & vendors, and increase sales.

My expertise & uniqueness adds value to my colleagues and employer (and/or customers) by providing...

5+ years of experience in the field of Marketing, and maintaining a positive attitude even during very stressful times. I pride myself on working hard, avoiding office gossip, being a true team player, being a creative thinker, staying focused on problem-solving, being honest and consistent, and having fun at work.

This helps them (colleagues, employer and/or customers) to....

Feel more comfortable knowing they can rely on me to deliver what is promised and they can trust that my personality/temperament will be consistent in any given situation(s).

As a result they...

Have a more positive experience whenever they collaborate/engage with me. This also helps my colleagues and vendors be more productive and enjoy their work more...

...than if they did <u>not</u> work with me.

My unique professional philosophy at work is offering...

A more authentic, personal, trustworthy, fun and consistent approach...

...than (some) others who are in the professional workforce.

Exercise 1: Your Turn! Your Core Uniqueness & Value Add:

START WITH LISTING 3-5 QUALITIES THAT MAKE YOU UNIQUE

1.

2.

3.

4.

5.

Now complete the following sentences with your own info, and you can refer to the example provided above:

The core purpose of my expertise and role at work is...

My expertise & uniqueness adds value to my colleagues and employer (and/or customers) by providing...

This helps them (colleagues, employer and/or customers) to....

As a result they...

...than if they did not work with me.

My unique professional philosophy at work is offering...

...than (some) others who are in the professional workforce.

STEP TWO: How to Define Your Brand Personality

STEP TWO OVERVIEW: Once you know the big picture about your Personal Leadership Brand from Step One, it's time to apply a *personality* to your personal brand. That means you'll need to define how you want your brand to be perceived in a unique way.

Here's an example: Apple Computers, Inc. is cool and hip. Period. And that type of *brand personality* permeates into everything they do: The company website, their ad campaigns, even their product development. And I don't just mean how cool their products are from an innovation standpoint; I'm also referring to the *physical* (industrial) design of them. Their products *look* cool.

Heck, Steve Jobs, the (sadly) now deceased Founder & CEO, even looked cool. He did global product announcements in jeans, black turtlenecks and sneakers, not expensive business suits. Steve Jobs wearing expensive business suits just wouldn't map to *who* he was (meaning, his Personal Leadership Brand!).

This is also a good time to think about your personal *visual* brand. What do I mean by that? Here are a few examples to illustrate this: Donald Trump and his hair (he *knows* it is part of his brand, big time); Ellen DeGeneres' sneakers, funky clothes and dancing; Michael Jackson's infamous sequined single glove; and, again, Steve Jobs' jeans, sneakers and black turtlenecks.

You can consider a *visual brand element* that will make you stand out and memorable. Let's say you love the color red. You could be known for always wearing red shirts/blouses, or red pants, or red shoes, or red socks, red ties, or red hats. *At the end of this chapter I'll share a true story about how silly socks catapulted one employee's brand...and her career!*

STEP TWO EXERCISE: It's Your Turn! Now Define Your Brand Personality

MY BRAND IS: Make a list of descriptive words (adjectives) like the examples provided. Don't go 'plain vanilla.' Get creative and go Technicolor!

PERSONAL LEADERSHIP BRAND PERSONALITY EXAMPLES:

STEVE JOBS: Cool, hip, cutting-edge, resourceful, irreverent, innovative

OPRAH: Honest, friendly, reliable, caring, hard-working, humorous, trustworthy

ELLEN: Funny, sincere, playful, honest, compassionate, wacky, smart, warm

DONALD TRUMP: Serious, ambitious, tough, fair, hard-working, caring, shrewd

SIR RICHARD BRANSON: Adventurous, confident, risk-taker, innovative, unique

DESCRIBE YOUR PERSONAL LEADERSHIP BRAND *PERSON-ALITY*:

MY PERSONAL LEADERSHIP BRAND PERSONALITY IS:

1.
2.
3.
4.
5.
6.
7.

STEP THREE: How to Create Your Personal Leadership Brand Positioning Statement

STEP THREE OVERVIEW: Okay. Now it's time to bring everything from Step One and Step Two together into a cohesive Personal Branding Positioning Statement. Your Positioning Statement becomes the foundation for your branding efforts: visual, written, physical and verbal. It's not meant to read like a clever headline on an ad. It is supposed to be a straightforward statement that defines the essence of your personal leadership brand – who you are and your point of differentiation. This will make more sense when you read the examples below!

The Formula to Follow:

"**I want to be known for being** *(adjectives that describe you)* **so that I can** *(brand promise of your goals <u>versus</u> the brand promise of <u>who you are</u>).*"

Example:

"**I want to be known for being** <u>*honest, fun, respectful, supportive, hard-working and innovative*</u> **so that I can** <u>*deliver effective results and solutions for my employer, my team, and my peers.*</u>"

WRITE (3) OPTIONS FOR YOUR PERSONAL LEADERSHIP BRAND!

Note: I know senior executives who post their Personal Branding Statement on the wall in their office because they want everyone to know what they stand for, and they ask people to "call them out" on anything they say or do that's not consistent with their brand platform.

Live Your Brand

Your Personal Leadership Brand is now complete...or is it? Test it to make certain you can live up to your brand *promise*. Do you have the ability to translate the qualities you articulate in your Personal Brand Positioning Statement into your day-to-day behavior? Can you commit to live the brand you are and/or aspire to be? Can you translate it into the decisions and choices you make daily?

Pose the following questions to see if it needs to be refined:

- Is this the brand identity that best represents who I am and what I can do?

- If I "live" this brand declaration, will I consider myself a success?

- Am I willing to tell others that this is my Personal Leadership Brand?

- Is this brand identity something that creates value in the eyes of my organization and key stakeholders?

- Is this brand true to who I am and/or aspire to be?

This last question is an important one...and the answer can be a trap for many employees. It can be tempting to choose a brand identity that supports organizational values, but not your own personal values and strengths. Some people believe that a *company-focused* Personal Leadership Brand will make them seem more valuable to the organization. *But this premise is wrong.*

Your Personal Leadership Brand must be true to who you are and not about what your employer may want to hear. Your brand is something that you should be able to *take with you* to a new company or position, and have it still be accurate. It's about who you are as a person and professional, not whom you believe *a company or boss* wants you to be.

If you follow that silly path, you'll be changing "who you are" (your brand) every time you get a new job or supervisor. That's ridiculous!

Here's a quick (true) story to illustrate that point: I had mentioned earlier in this chapter how knowing your brand can help you with choosing a job...I know a woman who was employed, but was offered a significant promotion and pay increase from another company. However, she turned it down and all of her friends (and husband!) thought she was nuts. So why did she? Because that company's culture, as well as the new boss she'd report to, didn't map to *her* Personal Brand. She knew that within a short period of time she'd probably be miserable there and have to start looking for another job.

Therefore, rather than jumping on the promotion and more money, she knew that if she kept job searching, the same type of offer, from a company she'd be happier at, with a new boss that she'd enjoy working for, would come along. And, eventually it did!

Do you know how many people accept new job offers JUST because of money or to get a new "bigger" title, and then regret it? A lot. I talk to them all the time. And I normally determine pretty fast it was because they were *not at all* clear on their Personal Branding, so they were making poor (career) decisions...yet they had NO idea why.

I think it's pretty amazing how effective Personal Branding cannot only propel your career, but that it can also simplify your life in ways you never imagined!

Lisa's Closing Comments:

The concept of developing a Personal Brand at work is not new, but it's *now* becoming a key component of management and leadership training. Companies, coaches, and consultants are working more and more with employees to help them better understand who they are, what they stand for, and how they want to be perceived. It really does nothing but positively impact the workplace when you have a lot of people who know who they are, who they aspire to be, and really know who their co-workers are! *Right???*

But before I end this chapter, here is the story about silly socks that I had promised to tell you as another example of adopting a "visual" brand element...

I know a young Millennial woman who was an engineer at a VERY large corporation with a brand name you'd probably know. But, aside from standing out as a woman in her department (because most all of the other engineers were men), she wanted something more that reflected her Personal Brand "personality". Keep in mind one her values was "having fun at work".

So she started to wear wild socks to the office with her very nice business attire, EVERY DAY. Word spread and then people, even people she didn't know, started to give her hilarious, weird socks at work. Seriously, she had a never-ending supply of socks being dropped off in her cubicle all the time.

This then led to her taking pictures of the socks she put on each morning and posting them on a very simple blog she created. And along with the sock picture each day, she'd also include a funny one-liner joke or an inspirational quote. This took her less than 5-minutes each morning to do, and people all over the company started sharing the link to her blog, posting comments, etc. And, wisely, a picture of her (not just her socks) was on the blog so people started to recognize her when she was walking around campus. Brilliant.

Well, one day she was walking down the hall and she passed a Senior Vice President going the opposite direction, whom was not frequently seen cruising the hallways and whom probably would have taken years for her to meet (if ever). She politely said hello, he grunted, and then he stopped dead in his tracks and said, "Excuse me, aren't you the engineer who wears weird socks?"

She nervously nodded, and he asked, "Which ones do you have on today?"

She raised her pant leg a few inches, he cracked up, and then asked her if she was busy at the moment. To which she replied that she was just on her way to lunch, and he invited her to attend a planning meeting that he was walking to, RIGHT THEN, for a huge, high profile project. She quickly decided lunch could wait and went with him. And during their walk to the conference room he told her he'd heard about her blog and occasionally looked at.

By the end of that planning meeting, because of her contributions to what was being discussed, she was asked to be on the special project team…something her colleagues would have given anything to be invited on.

Yes, of course, she is respected for her intelligence, education and work ethic, but now even the CEO of a company with 10,000+ employees knows who she is, AND has her on his radar. He, the CEO, has actually asked her to show her socks and he's typically with other senior execs, so the exposure for her kept going. And she has been asked to be on many other special project teams because so many people in the company know who she is!

So, just by her taking the time to concentrate on her Personal Branding, this young woman got creative and thought of a "visual" element to support one of her key values (having fun at work) to standout…I'd say her strategy worked!

How to Promote You for Career Success

*"If you don't have a plan for yourself, you'll be
a part of someone else's."*

American Proverb

INTRODUCTION TO PART FOUR

Once you've developed your own Personal Leadership Brand positioning, it's time to promote YOU inside and (if you want) *outside*, of work! And for those of you *who are interested* in gaining more notoriety within your industry, and not just within your company, this is a key section for you.

Many employees feel uncomfortable "promoting" themselves, but it's important to do. And this doesn't mean *bragging*. That turns people off and reflects poorly on you. What I do mean is acting as your own *Publicist* to generate awareness for yourself. And, as you'll soon see, there are a wide variety of things you can do!

So, I'm going to keep this section intro short. Let's jump right into the strategies!

CHAPTER FIFTEEN

Promoting You at Work

Okay. You've created your Personal Leadership Brand and now you want to start attracting some notoriety. This is a good thing! However, it's an area where many employees who want to achieve extreme career success drop the ball.

Why? Because! Everyone gets busy and stuck in his or her department *silos*. It's very common, especially if you work for a larger company, to spend a vast majority of your time at work with your department colleagues and rarely expand outside of that world.

But if you want to achieve bigger career success and become more known throughout your company, there are things you need to do within your department and outside of it. Sometimes, just "doing your job", even if you're great at it, isn't going to be enough to get you where you REALLY want to go.

So let's look at some key strategies for you to consider…

Networking at the Office: If you work for a larger company that has internal networking groups or clubs (like Women in Leadership Group, an African American Diversity Group, a softball team, a running club, etc.), have you joined one that matches your interests? And if you have joined one, do you actively participate on a regular basis?

When I ask this question at my workshops not many hands go up. But this is a KEY strategy! You've got to leave *your department* and get to know people *all around the company*.

If you work for a company that doesn't have internal networking groups, when was the last time you coordinated some sort of networking mixer to bring people from ALL departments together for socializing? Don't wait for other people to do it…you do it!

Remember, this is to benefit *your* Personal Brand, so make the effort. People will appreciate your coordinating something fun for the company to participate in…and they don't have to know it is part of your own personal "publicity" strategy.

But aside from participating in internal networking groups or clubs or coordinating events, you can be proactive at introducing yourself to key people in other departments. I know a woman who was a middle-manager at a Fortune 500 company, that looked at the org chart for each department, contacted VP's in each one, and invited them individually to coffee. She simply said that she wanted to know more about their department and career paths, and would appreciate 30-minutes of their time.

And what was the result? Not ONE VP declined her offer, plus most of those coffee meetings lasted for more than an hour! That's significant face time, alone, with senior executives she would have probably never met otherwise.

Within a few months she knew most of the key VP's throughout the company, and more importantly, *they knew her.* This then led to many invitations to be on special projects outside of her department, invitations to events she would never have known about before, even job offers from other departments, and finding *internal* Mentors that she could seek advice and support from.

Yes, it took guts and time to do what she did, but the pay-off for building her Personal Brand within the company was huge!

Go Out of Your Way to Help Others: If someone asks for volunteers on a project, or help with something they're struggling with, or even help with cleaning the break room, do it! I don't care what level on the org chart you are; if you're capable and qualified to do what is being asked, do it. It will reflect well on you in a variety of ways and that is important.

Why? Most people WON'T do it because in our own little minds we think we're the busiest people on the planet and don't have time to volunteer for something else. Well, the reality is that most of us DO have the time, *we simply choose not to make the time.*

Present Ideas Creatively: Don't be the person who puts people to sleep when you do presentations. One of the best things you can do for your Personal Brand is become known as a great presenter. And if you know this is an area you struggle with, hire a Speaking Coach to help you or join a local Toast Masters group in your area to get help and feedback on your skills.

I know employees who have worked on their presentation skills, became very good over time, and were then asked to do major, high-profile presentations because their boss(s) knew they would do a better job than s/he would. That is huge exposure!

No one likes a boring presentation. I'm not saying you have to juggle and tell jokes. I'm saying you need to have great content and confidence, which creates *rapport and presence*. Whether you have to do a presentation for 10 minutes to your co-workers and boss at your Monday morning meeting, or conduct a 45-minute presentation to 200+ people, always make it exceptional. Be prepared, practice a lot, and again, get help with your presentation skills if you need it. Great speakers have magnetism and being one greatly benefits your Personal Leadership Brand.

Promote Your News: Did you win an award from a club or org you belong to outside of work? Did you write an article that got published? Did you accomplish something cool like do a marathon? If so, share your news! And if your company has an internal company-wide e-newsletter, send them your news!

You never know who could read about it or hear about it, and then may want to reach out to you because they share a similar interest. Maybe a Sr. Vice President (whom you may not otherwise meet) is planning to train for a marathon next year, and she wants to pick your brain about your training and marathon experience… and who knows where THAT new connection could lead you!

Pat Others on the Back: Do not hold back compliments and kudos. And always share them publicly versus waiting until you're alone with the person. Also, if you know of something a co-worker has done that is exceptional, or went "above and beyond" to get a project done and no one else knows the extra effort they put in, announce it in meetings and/or send out mass emails sharing the news. No one will forget you did that for them, others will think it's admirable, and that could lead to people doing it for you at some point...and all of that supports the positive building of your Personal Brand.

Speaking at Work: Are there internal company events where you could think of a presentation topic and submit it for consideration? I'm sure there is. Every big company has events throughout the year (departments or company-wide) where they look for employees to speak at. And if you work for a smaller company that doesn't have internal events, you can create your own. Think of a topic that you know would help others at work or in their personal lives, and do a Brown Bag Lunch session. You can do this if you work for a large company, too!

For an internal presentation the topic you create doesn't even have to be around your "work" expertise. For example: If you practice meditation for stress reduction, but your "job" is as a Software Developer, who cares? You can promote a Brown Bag Lunch session where you'll share tips and strategies to reduce stress through meditation. You can promote it company-wide and attract ALL types of employees, from all different career levels, who think the topic is interesting. And, by them attending it, they will then get to know "who" you are and "what" you do in your role at the company. See? Now those who wouldn't otherwise have a reason to know you at work *will know you!*

Write, Write and Write: Contribute articles to your company's e-newsletter or blog. And if your company doesn't have either, think about creating a private blog that can only be accessed by employees of your company and post interesting and/or helpful information there. Or, create your own e-newsletter that you distribute to employees! You can compile links to articles you read pertaining to work and the industry, and simply email the list out once a month.

The goal here is to position you as a *Thought Leader* at your company. And it's okay if the info you share isn't always YOUR own custom content from your brain. By sharing the content of others that you find, as long as it's good, reflects well on you as a Thought Leader because you researched and found the info to share. It makes you a valuable information source at work and that will bolster your Personal Brand!

Be Uncomfortable: If you want to become more high profile at work, get out of your comfort zone and challenge yourself. And if you want to do this but you're too scared to make the move, get into therapy, get a Life Coach, or read self-help books, and take baby steps. Do whatever you need to do to build your confidence.

Just pick ONE strategy that was shared so far and start with it. You gotta start somewhere…and no one is going to do it for you.

But before we close this chapter, I'd like to leave you with a few questions to ask yourself one a regular basis. I have clients who actually have these questions on their mobile devices and review them at the end of each week as a way to "stay in touch" with themselves. Why? Because they care about their Personal Brands and they look at these questions as *a tool to manage* their brands actively…

On a Weekly Basis Honestly Ask Yourself:

1. What More Can I Offer at Work?

2. Do I, or Did I, Go Beyond What's in My Job Description?

3. How Productive & Innovative Was I? Can I Be More So?

4. How Do, or Did, My Work & Ideas Add to the Bottom Line?

5. Are My Daily, Weekly and Monthly Contributions Essential?

6. Do My Actions Inside of Work and Outside of Work Truly Support My Career Goals? And…Am I Willing to Do More?

For the questions above that warrant a yes/no answer, if you didn't answer *YES* to all of them, you're negatively impacting your Personal Brand and sabotaging your career success! If you answer "no" to them a lot, it could be that you don't like your job, boss, or company...and if that's the case, then it's time to move on. Because when you're clear on your Personal Brand, then you gain clarity on your career goals, and that helps you decide what job or project "fits" with *what* you want, *who* you are, and who you *aspire* to be.

Lisa's Closing Comments:

If you want to stand out at work in a positive way and get more recognition within your department and/or companywide, you HAVE to make an effort to "be known". And, even if you're amazing at your *job*, there's a good chance the only people who are going to know that are the colleagues you have regular contact with.

The bottom line to *expand your brand* outside of your department silo is to become your own "Publicist" by trying one, or many, of the strategies shared in this chapter. And I'm assuming you want more recognition throughout your company or you wouldn't be reading this book...*so go for it!*

CHAPTER SIXTEEN
Promoting You to the Industry

I hope that the previous chapter has your head spinning with great ideas for promoting your Personal Brand at work! Now, let's discuss strategies for promoting yourself *outside* of your workplace. However, before we get started, I do want to share some <u>very important</u> advice with you. Prior to embarking on your self-promotion efforts to your industry or the world, be sure to check with your employer on their policies pertaining to things like Social Media, PR, publishing articles, and Public Speaking.

Some larger corporations have strict policies for these things and you could find yourself in a lot of trouble with your company's Legal Department if you break their rules. The reason for this is that anything you do that mentions the company *also reflects on the company's brand*. As long as you work *for* them, you're a representative *of* them. This means that you may have to submit articles you write to your Legal, Corporate Communications, or PR Departments before you can submit them to an industry magazine or blog you want it published in.

This may also be required for any public speaking you want to do at industry conferences or tradeshows. Many large corporations have strict legal policies on this, and some even require their employees to go through their internal "speaker" training before you can speak publicly as a *representative of the company*.

That said, I have found that most (smart) employers are thrilled to have employees writing articles for industry publications/blogs, speaking at industry events, and conducting interviews with industry media, because it gives them (the employer) more exposure for their brand, too (at it doesn't cost your employer anything!).

Just make sure you do your homework on everything mentioned above to avoid any unpleasant results. The last thing you want is to get fired or sued because you didn't follow the company's protocol. Right?

Allllrighhhtyyy then, enough of my words of caution…let's talk about the fun stuff!

Networking (*Outside of the Office*): This is similar to joining networking groups AT work. How many professional groups do you belong to outside of the office? There are networking groups in every city for just about any industry or profession you can think of, and you need to join appropriate ones for you and actively participate.

I'm always shocked at the workshops I conduct by how many employees don't participate in networking groups *outside* of the office! If you're a woman, join an organization for professional women. If you're a Marketing Manager, join your local Marketing and/or Advertising Club. If you're the Director of HR, join your local HR Association.

Investing just 1-2 evenings or lunch hours <u>per month</u> to attend these types of professional networking gatherings is HUGE for building your Personal Brand! Not only will they help you stay current on new research and trends in your industry or profession, you'll meet all kinds of people who know *all kinds of people.* You can also learn about events where you can speak, contribute articles to the organization's blog or newsletter, volunteer for high-profile committees, find a Mentor (outside of your company) that can support you professionally, and much more!

Meetup Groups: At the time of this writing, Meetup groups are active everywhere across the country and there are tons to choose from! You can search for ones that are specific to your personal interests too, such as, "Millennials Who Love Wine". You can meet other professionals in your age group, build relationships with them, and do it over a common interest…like chardonnay or cabernet!

Another strategy to consider is to start your own Meetup group. Let's say you're a female executive in your 50's who lives in Seattle and you're having a tough time finding a professional organization that you enjoy attending...even if you are a member of one, you can still start your OWN group. For instance, you can form a Meetup group called "Professional Boomer Women of Seattle". Be sure to promote your Meetup group at work and that will generate more notoriety for you there, too!

Align With Others Who Share Your Values: Your Personal Brand means nothing if you surround yourself with people who don't share your values and goals. If part of your branding is to be known as someone who doesn't get involved in negative office politics then don't hang out with people who gossip and cause problems at work. And that goes for outside of the office, too!

Focus on building a network of professional colleagues who have Personal Brands that align with yours. They will introduce you to others whom you can relate to and the domino effect will occur. Successful (emotionally healthy) professionals don't waste their valuable time networking with people who can "drag them down". And I'm not referring to them being snobby about another person's profession or income. Emotionally healthy people care about who someone is *as a person*, not just about what someone does *for a living*.

Basically, successful professionals are intolerant of people who bring little more than drama, or an "all about me" attitude, to the table.

So, if this requires you to clean house of some friends you have, or co-workers you socialize with, do it. Get clear on *whom* you are and *what* you value, and only surround yourself with people who are like-minded.

Therefore, the big question becomes, "Is who you are and what you value, *healthy?*" And I'm sure you've (possibly) seen enough Reality TV to understand the point I'm trying to make here, but it's relative. Some people value being greedy, others don't. Some people value helping others, some people don't.

Note: I know some very successful, wealthy, executives who are the nicest people in the world, and everyone they surround themselves with are also wonderful. So, you don't have to be a schmuck to get ahead. The choice is yours.

Actively Blog: To establish *you* as a Thought Leader, starting a blog (or podcast/vidcast) is a key tool to consider for your self-promotion toolbox. Obviously for legal reasons you don't want to chat about "private" things your company is doing or projects that you're working on at work, but you <u>can</u> discuss industry trends, provide educational "how to" info, and discuss news and events that pertain to your industry. Plus, you can offer your opinions about those things to showcase your *Thought Leader* expertise.

One idea: You can attend an industry tradeshow and conduct a short interview with a keynote speaker at the event, record it on video, and post it on your blog. A short 3-5 minute interview with someone who is considered a "player" in your industry will give you credibility just for interviewing him or her.

Or, ask a big fish in your industry to write a guest article for your blog. Again, just by being associated with them can heighten *your* credibility and notoriety!

Having an active blog can attract industry media and other industry Thought Leaders to you, as well as it can build your brand awareness so that you're contacted for speaking engagements and article writing opportunities.

Another key tip here is to also participate on other industry blogs by posting comments. You need to take some time to share your expertise and knowledge on other peoples' blog to generate traffic to *your* blog!

Note: This general blogging strategy also works for doing your own podcast or BlogTalk Radio show. Find experts to interview, post the recording, and you can build your brand by being the "host" of your own show.

Social Media: Aside from blogging and podcasts, you can also consider the following online strategies. But let me just say that my intention here is not to go into detail about "how" to do these things and not to provide you with marketing strategies to promote them. Although I do discuss those topics with my clients and in my workshops, blog, Facebook Page, and articles, my goal here is to simply tell you the mediums to consider. From there, you can research the "ins & outs" of the ones you are interested in implementing. Here are a few to consider:

• **YouTube:** Start your own YouTube Channel and post short videos pertaining to industry news, trends and events. You can also post short interviews with other industry experts AND key employees at your company. That would help generate more notoriety for you and your channel at work!

• **Facebook Business Page:** This is the same concept as a YouTube Channel. Make it all about your industry and profession, and post good info that educates your target audience. Also, join other Facebook Pages that relate to your industry and profession and participate in those online communities, too.

• **LinkedIn:** Make sure your Profile is current, and make sure you have integrated popular keywords into your Profile's text so that your chance of being found through online search improves. LinkedIn Profiles are searchable on Google, so if someone is doing keyword searches that relate to you and your expertise, your Profile will show up in their search results. As with Facebook Business Pages, you can join LinkedIn Groups in your industry, or start your own Group, or do both! The key here, as with any Social Media community, is to participate on a regular basis. It's just like joining in-person professional networking associations in your city or town…if you don't attend their events, you don't benefit!

Articles & Interviews: Create a list of industry blogs, newspapers, magazines, Fan Pages, radio shows, TV shows, podcast, etc. that target your audience and industry, and contact them with article ideas and segment topics.

Public Speaking: This is the same concept as writing articles, but you need to create a list of industry conferences and tradeshows to pitch your speaking topics to. Most of them will have "Submission for Proposal" info on their websites that will explain the types of topics they want for their event, submission guidelines, submission deadlines, etc. However, if you don't see that info on their website, contact the Event Manager and get the info.

When you first get started speaking, you'll have to do a lot of outreach. However, once you've done several speaking engagements, and have implemented some of the other self-promotion strategies we've discussed up to this point, you'll see an uptick in Event Planners contacting you to speak at their events. Plus, if you work at a large company, they may reach out to your company asking them to provide a speaker for their event. So you need to become one of the employees that your PR Department or Corporate Communications Department has on their list of internal speakers to recommend.

Note: I know many large corporations who require employees to go through their internal speaker training "certification" program before they are allowed to speak at events. Therefore, if you work for a big company, make sure to research their policies about this and follow the proper steps.

Write a Book: I know this may seem daunting to many of you, but you can do it quickly and easily if you want to! And if you don't want to write it yourself, then hire a ghostwriter to do the heavy lifting for you. Also, you don't have to bother with landing a book deal with a Publisher. This typically requires you to land a Literary Agent first, and that can be a lengthy process. So, my advice is to just self-publish it!

I could go on and on about writing a book and how to do it, and I help clients with this all the time and conduct workshops about it. But I'm not going to dive into those details here.

All you have to know is that there are simple and inexpensive ways to get a book written and published, and the credibility that you'll get from doing it can be a game-changer for you. Writing a book is a powerful tool to consider for building your Personal Brand, plus it can generate revenue *for you* from book sales, increase media interest *in you*, AND attract (paid) speaking engagements *to you.*

PR: This is a big topic and one that you definitely need to communicate with your internal PR Department, boss, or company owner about. Writing Press Releases and deploying them to industry media and through online services (like PRWeb.com) is critical for building your Personal Brand *outside* of your company. But you want to get approval to do it.

A Press Release is important when you write an e-book, a Special Report, a book, or get invited to speak at an industry conference, because you obviously want to promote this news to the masses. But, again, because you are an employee and your Personal Brand is tied to your *employer's brand*, they get a say in what you write and how it's written.

So if your company does have a PR Department, external PR Agency, or even just one person who is responsible for Marketing and PR internally, you want to create a strong relationship with them. They may even be able to help you craft your Press Releases and help you distribute them.

Once you have a Press Release written, share the link to it through your Social Media networks and on your blog. Plus, when those Press Releases are picked up in industry media, you can share the links to the articles you're quoted in as well as links to any "broadcast" interviews where you're the featured guest expert (i.e. podcasts, vidcasts, radio or TV).

Website: Ideally, you can have your own "Thought Leader" website (where you clearly state where you work), but if your employer isn't comfortable with that, you can use *your blog* as the "go to" place that you drive traffic to. For example, when you distribute a Press Release, write an article, or do a guest blog post for someone else, you'll want to have your website or blog's web address in your byline/bio info at the end so people can learn more about you.

Your personal website or blog is where you can post about: media coverage you've gotten, Press Releases you've written, speaking engagements you've booked, e-books or books you've written, podcasts you've done, etc. Basically, you need to have an online "depository" for everything about you.

Note: If your employer also has a problem with you even having a blog, then you can simply make your LinkedIn Profile the "for more information about me" destination you drive traffic to.

Lisa's Closing Comments:

If you were self-employed, this would be a no-brainer. Many of my one-on-one consulting and coaching clients are so we don't have to worry about employer "rules" with the marketing strategies I develop for them. But, because *you are* an employee, you need to get approval from your employer or you could face some major legal problems. My hope, however, is that because your intention is to *clearly state where you're employed* in everything that you do in your external self-promotion efforts, *which means you're also getting your employer's brand more exposure through your efforts,* they won't have a problem with your path.

It may take some extra time to follow company protocol, and require you to jump through hoops that you'd prefer not to, but the end results will be very positive for you. And if your employer realizes this is a win-win situation, and doesn't feel like you're doing this just to *leave them,* you have a very good chance of getting their support.

Info Lisa Wants to Share

"Every day employees all over the world, in a wide variety of jobs, at a wide variety of career-levels, complain that they are not experiencing the success they desire. And typically that's because they haven't made the effort to really understand 'themselves', make necessary changes to weaknesses they may have, nor focus on creating a unique presence & style that sets them apart from their workforce peers. Don't let that be you! Take control of your future and make the extra effort to standout! No one is going to do it for you."

Lisa Orrell
Author of this book, Mom to Jenner, BBQ Queen, Wine Fan,
Professional Speaker, Coach & Consultant

CHAPTER SEVENTEEN

How Lisa Can Help You: Presentations & Coaching

SEMINARS & WORKSHOPS OFFERED BY LISA:

Audiences unanimously agree that Lisa's presentation style is fast, fun, energetic, and witty, with a heavy concentration on *EDU*-TAINMENT. What does THAT mean? Attendees come away with interesting insights but find themselves totally entertained in the process!

Lisa adds new, innovative, timely topics to her presentation offerings regularly, so visit her website or contact her for more information. She can also provide you with her Presentations Overview Package that outlines each topic in more detail, along with pricing. Plus, Lisa can customize any of her presentations to fit your needs, your industry, and/or your event's allocated program schedule. Client References are available upon request.

SEMINAR TITLES
(These can also be presented as Webinars):

1. Get A Grip on Gen Y: How to Recruit, Manage, Motivate and Retain Our New (Unique!) Generation of Young Professionals *(for anyone, including College Faculty, responsible for recruiting, managing, and/or teaching Millennials)*

2. Get A Grip On Leadership: Empowering Millennial Employees to Adopt a Leadership Mindset at Work *(for Millennial Employees or College Students)*

3. Global Millennials: Insights Into Our First Global Generation & Their Impact on Employers Worldwide...Now and in the Future! *(for mid-to-senior level Executives)*

4. Understanding Generations for Sales Acceleration *(for Sales Teams)*

5. Improving Communication Across the Generations *(for Employees of all generations)*

WORKSHOP TITLES:

1. Your Personal Brand is in Your Hands: How to Create a Personal Leadership Brand for Career Success *(for Employees of all generations and career levels…and it's also a perfect topic for High School & College Students!)*

2. Millennial Business Boot Camp: Everything You Need to Know to Be a Respected Young Professional *(for Millennial Employees & College Students)*

3. Transitioning to Leadership Program: How to Effectively Move Your Millennial Employees Into Leadership Roles *(co-facilitated with Camille Smith, President of Work In Progress Coaching, Inc., and a 25-year Executive & Leadership Coach)*

KEYNOTES:

Lisa's keynotes can be conducted for professionals of all levels, in any industry, from all generations…and her messages are also ideal for High School and College Students! Get in touch with Lisa for more information and to discuss her being a Keynote Speaker for you.

MODERATOR, PANELIST & BREAK-OUT SESSIONS:

On a regular basis Lisa is invited to moderate panel discussions, be a guest Panelist, and conduct Break-Out Sessions at Corporate and Association events. Therefore, if you are looking for a lively, entertaining, and knowledgeable expert for your next event be sure to contact her!

LEADERSHIP & CAREER COACHING:

Lisa is a *Certified* Leadership Coach for Millennials and Gen X'ers who value personal growth, want to excel in their careers, and who want to accelerate their path to professional and personal fulfillment. But if you don't understand the "benefits" of working with a Professional Coach yet, just being open to it means you're on the right track!

A majority of respected senior executives, C-level professionals, world leaders, premier athletes, and successful entrepreneurs, hire "personal support" Coaches for a variety of reasons. Why? They benefit from it.

However some people are confused about what professional coaching *is and is not.* Coaching is not therapy, counseling or psychotherapy. Lisa's role as your personal Leadership & Career Coach is to be your guide and partner, and utilize her skills, knowledge, experience, and professional coach training to help you overcome obstacles to exceed your own expectations.

There are a wide range of Coaches: Life Coaches, Executive Coaches, Financial Coaches, Small Business Coaches, Leadership Coaches, Relationship Coaches, Career Coaches, etc. But regardless of their niche, Lisa believes they all have 2 things in common:

1. They work with people who are already in a healthy "emotional" place in their lives (or who are also working with a Therapist to work through "heavier" issues), but that want to continue growing and excelling – personally and/or professionally.

2. "Life coaching" is a component of ANY type of coaching. It's all about YOU and YOUR life, so how couldn't it be?

Lisa's Role as Your Leadership & Career Coach is To:

- Help you *uncover* your goals, roadblocks, opportunities, and vision

- Build and/or maintain *your confidence* to achieve your goals

- Create a plan to help *you achieve* your short-term & long-term goals faster

- Provide effective feedback that *supports* your goals, objectives and vision

- Provide you with a *safe and confidential* space to be open, grow, share & learn

- Assist you with *making decisions,* keep you on track, evaluate your choices & give you clarity

- Bring out *your strengths* and overcome your weaknesses

- Not be your "yes" woman, but provide you with *honest feedback and insights*

- *Remain objective* & approach your working relationship without judgment, criticism or bias

- Help you become the exceptional leader, and person, *you envision*

- Be *your sounding board* when faced with challenges at work (or in your personal life), and provide you with effective feedback

- Make sure you both *have a lot of fun* throughout the process!

To learn more about Lisa's Coaching Services and how she can benefit you, visit her website. There's an entire Coaching Section that can answer many of your questions: TheOrrellGroup.com.

RESOURCES:

No matter your generation or career level, here is a short list of (classic & timeless) business books that Lisa recommends to help you excel professionally. They can all support you in becoming the effective leader you aspire to be…as well as provide you with great tools to build your *positive* Personal Leadership Brand:

The 21 Irrefutable Laws of Leadership, by John C. Maxwell

The 360° Leader: Developing Your Influence from Anywhere in the Organization, by John C. Maxwell

Leading From The Heart: Choosing to be a Servant Leader, by Jack Kahl

The Heart of a Leader: Insights on the Art of Influence, by Ken Blanchard

Make Their Day! Employee Recognition That Works, by Cindy Ventrice

1501 Ways to Reward Employees, by Bob Nelson Ph.D.

Lisa Orrell, CPC
The Generations Relations & Leadership Expert
SPEAKER • TRAINER • CERTIFIED LEADERSHIP COACH
AUTHOR • THOUGHT LEADER

Lisa@TheOrrellGroup.com
1-888-254-LISA
www.TheOrrellGroup.com

Join Lisa Online:
Twitter @GenerationsGuru • Facebook • LinkedIn • YouTube

ABOUT THE AUTHOR

Lisa Orrell, CPC
The Generations Relations & Leadership Expert
SPEAKER • TRAINER • CERTIFIED LEADERSHIP COACH
AUTHOR • THOUGHT LEADER

Lisa Orrell is globally recognized as The Generations Relations & Leadership Expert, and she's the award-winning author of *four* business books on Amazon: *Millennials Incorporated; Millennials into Leadership; Boomers into Business;* and her latest book, *Your Employee Brand is in Your Hands.*

She's an in-demand speaker and consultant hired by many well-known organizations, such as (partial list): Wells Fargo, Johnson & Johnson, Intuit, Pepsi, Applied Materials, Paul Mitchell Schools, eBay/PayPal, Cisco, USC's Marshall School of Business, Monster.com, and Blue Cross/BlueShield.

As a speaker and consultant, Lisa conducts a variety of dynamic seminars, workshops and keynotes that: Improve generation relations at work; educate Leadership Teams on employee-related workforce trends; improve the recruitment, management and retention of Millennial (aka: Gen Y) Talent; and that educate Millennial employees & college students on how to be effective young leaders in the workforce. She also conducts popular *Personal Branding* workshops for employees to support their career growth and leadership development (with audiences often ranging in age from 21 – 60+ years old).

Lisa is also a Certified Leadership Coach that works with Millennial and Gen X employees, entering or currently in, a leadership role at work. She received her Leadership Coaching Certification through an intensive training program accredited by the International Coach Federation.

Prior to her current career, Lisa owned a full-service Marketing Agency in the San Francisco Bay Area for 20-years, and her company received over 75 national and international awards for Marketing & Branding excellence. Plus, over 22,000 industry professionals recently named her one of the "Top 30 Most Influential Branding Gurus in the World". She holds a Bachelor's Degree in Advertising with a Minor in Marketing from San Jose State University.

And because of her vast Marketing experience and background, Lisa has another business as *The Promote U Guru* (PromoteUGuru.com). As such, she is a highly regarded Branding Expert, Marketing Consultant, and Business Coach who works with individual clients, including: business professionals, entrepreneurs, small business owners, coaches, consultants, entertainers, academics, speakers, and authors.

Based on her topic expertise and notoriety in both areas of her professional life, Lisa has been interviewed by, or written articles for, countless media and research firms, including (partial list): ABC, NPR, MSNBC, CBS, *The NY Times, Wall Street Journal, TIME, Cosmo, U.S. News & World Report, Human Resource Executive, The Business Journals* (throughout the U.S.), *Women's Health, Recruitment & Retention,* Universum's *Trainee Guides* for Norway, Sweden and Denmark, China's *HerWorld* Magazine, *Diversity Business, Latino University* Magazine, *Black Enterprise,* HR.com, FoxBusiness.com, BNET.com, Monster.com, Entrepreneur.com, and CareerBuilder.com.

CPSIA information can be obtained
at www.ICGtesting.com
Printed in the USA
FSOW03n1404100915
10890FS